ORGANIZATION DEVELOPMENT FOR OPERATING MANAGERS

ORGANIZATION DEVELOPMENT FOR OPERATING MANAGERS

Michael E. McGill

amacom

A DIVISION OF AMERICAN MANAGEMENT ASSOCIATIONS

Library of Congress Cataloging in Publication Data

McGill, Michael E
    Organization development for operating managers.

    Includes index.
    1. Organizational change. I. Title.
HD58.8.M23   658.4'06   76-50051
ISBN 0-8144-5381-3

© 1977 AMACOM

A division of American Management Associations, New York.
All rights reserved. Printed in the United States of America.

First Printing

This book

is dedicated to

Janet, Jimmy, and Adam

they give purpose and perspective

to all that I do

Foreword

Operating managers need information and advice about a relatively new practice, organization development (OD). *Organization Development for Operating Managers* addresses this need. Its purpose is to inform and to advise: to inform operating managers about OD and the alternative approaches to OD and to advise them how to manage their choice.

The emergence at this time of the need for information and advice was predictable. There is a pattern to the popularity of managerial practices, one that is readily apparent to experienced observers of organizational life. What is fad one year is often fashion the next and function the following year. Moreover, this fad-fashion-function cycle seems to repeat about every ten years. Often it is accompanied by critics' claims that "only the names have been changed." So it was with executive development programs in the 1950s and management development programs in the 1960s. In each case the development programs were viewed initially as passing fads. Both in time became fashionable and are now looked upon as established organizational functions.

These observations may have the character of a truism, which makes it appear to some that I am belaboring the obvious. Yet the pattern deserves our attention since we appear to be in the midst of still another go-round, this time in behalf of organization development.

While OD differs in both focus and form from its predecessors (a point discussed at length in Chapter 1), there are indications that OD will follow a similar evolutionary pattern—maybe. Certainly OD programs were the fad in training and development in the late 1960s and there is ample evidence to suggest that OD efforts are now quite fashionable. Whether OD programs will complete the cycle and emerge as established organizational functions in the future is questionable, however. This doubt reflects, I think, the doubts in the minds of operating managers, the people ultimately responsible for the effectiveness and functionality of OD. The merits and faults of OD have been debated, discussed, and in some instances resolved by academics, consultants, and corporate-level executives in countless conferences, seminars, articles, and books. For the operating manager, however, many critical questions regarding OD remain unanswered. The operating managers' questions must be answered if OD's full potential is to be realized.

What are the critical questions operating managers ask? They were recently summarized for me by a close friend who is director of the marketing division of a national industrial chemicals company. He had heard that the president of his company, recently returned from a conference on OD, was thinking of embarking on a major OD effort. The president, it seems, was going to ask his divisional managers for their reactions, and my friend wanted to be able to respond intelligently. Explaining his dilemma to me, he said somewhat excitedly, "First, I don't even know what OD really is. But more than that — I feel that even when I know what it is I still won't know what it *means*. What does OD *really* do? And what do I do while OD is being done — to me, for me, or by me?"

Reflecting on his questions later in the evening, I thought that out of his own sense of ignorance and feelings of frustration, he had raised some questions which plague many operating managers. A quick check of other manager acquaintances confirmed this. Operating managers have a rapidly expanding awareness of the existence of ideas and practices which carry the label OD, but they lack an understanding of just what OD does or how one deals with it. Operating managers want descriptive data and prescriptive advice. They want to know just what forms OD takes and what uses it has. Operating managers want a description of OD in terms of their own experience, from their unique organizational perspective, so they may better understand what they hear and make intelligent choices for their own organizations. Operating managers need prescriptive plans for how to deal with OD. What role does the manager play in OD? How does he integrate an OD effort with his ongoing organizational activity? In short, how does he *manage* OD?

These are important questions about the aims and efforts of OD coming from people who are in positions to make or break OD. They want a description about it from their perspective, and they deserve a response. This book is meant to fill that need. Therefore the book is addressed to operating managers, although I hope others may find it interesting and helpful.

The book is a guide to OD, not a training manual. It describes alternative OD strategies and their uses in a manner that will help the operating manager make decisions about OD, and it offers a process for managing that effort.

Many individuals have contributed directly and indirectly to this book. I would like to thank my clients over the last seven years who have provided me with the opportunity to test my ideas in the laboratory of their organizations. Many of their stories, both the successes and the failures, are reflected in these pages.

Several operating managers have contributed to the book by keeping me in touch with the reality of their worlds and work. They have been my consultants throughout this project. My good friend Bob German has been particularly helpful. His candid sharing of his managerial experience with organizational change has been an enriching education for me.

Many of my colleagues have contributed to this book in numerous ways. Neely Gardner was and will always be my mentor in this field. Rick Ross has been an associate, a constant friend, and a source of stimulation. John Cutsinger, an accomplished trainer and OD consultant, provided the data for many of the cases. Gene Byrne, Fred Crandall, Craig Lundberg, Jim Tarter, and Mike Wooton, all fellow faculty members at the School of Business, Southern Methodist University, encouraged and stimulated my efforts over the many months this project consumed. The administration of the SBA–SMU also has my gratitude for their facilitation and encouragement of hands-on faculty involvement in operational business problems.

Jane Yoder typed the early drafts of the manuscript with skill and support that will always be to me a standard for how such work should be done.

My editors at AMACOM have been patient beyond reasonable limits throughout the project.

These many people made this book possible, but whatever shortcomings or errors may appear must rest with me. I bear the final responsibility for the accuracy and applicability of *Organization Development for Operating Managers*.

Mick McGill

Contents

CHAPTER 1

What Is OD?

What is OD? This question is heard more and more often among operating managers as they are exposed in literature and in practice to this new management process. Oddly enough, the same growth which prompts the question complicates the response. Popular management literature and practice by no means make OD clear. This confusion exists because its tremendous growth and expansion in recent years have been characterized more by divergence than by direction.

The field of OD has been populated by a multitude of consultants from various personal and professional backgrounds. They have employed an infinite variety of strategies to meet the needs of organizations of all descriptions. Observation of this OD activity has been easy for operating managers, because it has been all around them—if not in their own organizations, in those of their competitors. Making sense of it has been another matter. In seeking common properties from which he might draw generalizations about what OD is and how it works, the interested manager has confronted incidents which seem to have little more in common than the label itself. Brief descriptions of three separate organizations and their use of OD are presented to illustrate the point.

Case 1: Mahlen

Mike Mahlen is president of Mahlen's Maintenance, a custodial company serving the capital city of a rural southern state. Mahlen's company has contracts for custodial care of most of the major business and government buildings in the city. The firm employs approximately 100 custodians, 10 foremen, and 2 office workers. Salaries and workloads are consistent with those of similar companies in the area. Over the last three years, Mahlen's company has experienced an average annual turnover of 150 percent. In addition to the direct costs of recruitment and training, the turnover has adversely affected service and threatened the renewal of several key contracts. Mahlen contacted a consultant and began an OD program in hope of reducing turnover, improving service, and maintaining and increasing contracts.

Case 2: Paul

Bud Paul directs the recreation division of a large northwestern corporation. Paul's division owns and operates family recreational facilities in a seven-state area: motels, campgrounds, resort lakes, and so on. The division has grown greatly in the last two years through acquisition of smaller, independently owned and operated facilities. Due to the shortage of experienced recreational managers, many of the former owner-managers have been retained. Paul's division has profited greatly by these acquisitions, but there have been problems. As divisional director, Bud Paul feels that only he has a sense of corporate goals and a commitment to them. His separate facility managers (14 in all) seem to lack a concern for the total enterprise. They seldom enforce specific corporate policies. They interact with one another infrequently and with corporate representatives even less often. Paul is concerned that this lack of commitment will ultimately affect corporate growth, and he has initiated an OD program to remedy the situation.

Case 3: Kowalski

Pete Kowalski owns and manages a custom-molding plastics plant in the Great Lakes region. The plant is small, employing only 20 to 25 people at peak periods. Business is at an all-time high. Contracts have been signed for molding certain wood-substitute products. This development promises to increase the volume of the company fivefold over the next three years. Such growth will require expansion of equipment, employees, and managerial and organizational skills. Kowalski, concerned that his company begin now to plan for and meet the needs it will experience in the near future, has initiated an OD program to achieve this purpose.

These examples—differing in place, problem, purpose, and process (a point illustrated later in this chapter)—show where OD is used. One of the great difficulties managers find in learning about OD is that so many organizational processes can be, and are, included under that label. The problem in defining the field seems to lie not so much in the absence of definitions as in their abundance. Operating managers attempting to understand what OD is and how it works are all too often confused by the many conflicting concepts of OD, few of which are expressed in terms meaningful to managers. Frustrated at the first step, many managers carry their consideration no further.

Clarity must precede comprehension. Toward that end, this chapter first presents a definition of OD in terms meaningful to managers. Second, these terms are expanded and some popular misconceptions are exposed. Finally, the three cases introduced above are followed through to their conclusions, illustrating some of the kinds of problems to which OD is applied and some of the results.

DEFINING OD

Organization development is a conscious, planned process of developing an organization's capabilities so that it can attain and sustain an optimum level of performance as measured by efficiency, effectiveness, and health. Operationally, OD is a normative process of addressing the questions: "Where are we?" "Where do we want to be?" "How do we get from where we are to where we want to be?" This process is undertaken by members of the organization using a variety of techniques, often in collaboration with a behavioral science consultant.

This definition is necessarily lengthy. To attempt to understand OD by a shorthand definition focusing myopically on a single selected purpose or process is to deny its essential, comprehensive character. The simplicity of such definitions may be appealing, but they can be misleading. Although they contain some partial truths, they have promoted many misconceptions about OD which have misguided managers in their thinking.

A comprehensive definition, such as that provided above, satisfies managers' need to know *what* OD attempts to do, *how* it goes about it, and *who* is involved. A detailed explanation and examination of this definition, part by part, will clarify the meaning and dispel the misconceptions of OD for operating managers.

WHAT OD IS AND WHAT IT IS NOT

OD is a conscious, planned process. It is a purposeful organizational activity with a patterned relationship between its processes. Both participants and other organization members know what it is they're involved in and why.

OD is not simply planned organizational change. Perhaps the most common definition of OD is "planned organizational change." This broad perspective has been widely accepted by managers both because it sounds elementary and because it frames the field in terms of dynamics familiar to managers: planning and change.

This simplistic answer to OD misleads managers' thinking about the field in three significant ways. First, if OD is really nothing more than planned organizational change, then it offers nothing new. Any experienced operating manager has made a career of planning and implementing organizational changes. If that is all there is to OD, it has very little to offer operating managers. Many managers, believing OD to be nothing more than planned organizational change, have passed over the field because by this definition it offers very little new to them. Managers thus misled miss the opportunity OD offers.

Second, this misconception of OD as planned organizational change misguides managerial discussions and decisions about OD by unnecessarily broadening the field. If OD is viewed as planned organizational change, any and all planned change activity represents an OD effort and makes the field virtually boundless, encompassing nearly everything a manager does from the most minute personnel and technological changes to total systems concerns. Where OD means everything, it in fact means very little, and some mistaken managers thus understandably give it little attention.

Finally, the view of OD as simply planned organizational change has led many managers to castigate OD for promoting change for its own sake. In this perspective, the current popularity of OD is translated as the popularity of change. Many managers are rightfully suspicious that where change is fashionable it may not always be functional. Indeed, change made only in the interest of fashion is probably never functional. If change were the only purpose of OD and planning its only process, managers would be correct in viewing the field as more faddish than functional. The misdefinition of OD as mere organizational change has misled managers to a loss of interest in OD, which is regrettable for their organizations and for OD.

OD is a conscious planned process of developing an organization's capabilities so that it can attain and sustain an optimum level of performance as measured by efficiency, effectiveness, and health. These elements of the definition describe the aims and purposes of OD. They are important elements deserving expansion and emphasis.

Performance is a function of potential. Attaining and sustaining optimum performance requires organizational processes which allow people and programs to realize their full potential. These processes are the capabilities OD seeks to develop in an organization.

The need to attain and sustain optimum performance further delineates the target organizational capabilities. Too often, managers feel it necessary to "purchase"—that is, to hire—expertise or talents from outside the organization in order to optimize performance. Once the job is done, the outside talent and expertise leave the organization. Today's problems have been solved, but should new problems arise tomorrow, once again the organization would be faced with the necessity of bringing in outside help. Under this purchase model, optimum performance once attained cannot be sustained; it must each time be reattained at renewed cost. The aim of OD is to develop the organization's in-house capabilities—processes aiding realization of potential—to the point where optimum performance is regularly programmed rather than periodic and/or purchased.

OD measures optimum performance of an organization in terms of its efficiency, effectiveness, and health. Managers have long recognized that although profit and production are essential, they are not in themselves sufficient measures of organizational performance. Morale, creativity, and organization climate or atmosphere are all elements of a third category by which managers gauge both their own performance and that of their organizations. Broadly stated, this third dimension is organizational health, the locus of concerns for maximizing human potential and encouraging personal growth by management and employees alike.

Efficiency may be measured by the ratio of input to output, such as raw resources to finished goods. The general rule governing efficiency considerations is "mini-max": minimize inputs and maximize outputs. Effectiveness is less a quantitative dimension, like efficiency, than a qualitative one. Effectiveness is an organization's degree of achievement in reaching its goals — that is, the extent to which stated goals are reached. Effectiveness is for most organizations a "maxi-max" concern: maximize goals and maximize goal achievement.

Organizational health is a function of the character and quality of the relationship between individuals and the organization. A healthy organization is characterized in three important ways. First it effectively integrates individual and organizational goals. What people must do as organization members is consistent with what they feel they must do as individuals apart from the organization. Second, individual and organizational problem-solving capacities are maximized. Processes exist for the full exercise of people's potential, both as individuals and in groups. Finally, the climate encourages individual and organizational growth. Individuals and the organization are encouraged and aided in the discovery and development of their full potential.

Managers are well aware that the specific criteria of optimum performance differ from one organization to another. Yet, while the specifics may differ, the categories of performance criteria remain constant. In OD, progress is measured against optimum performance, *as defined by the manager and the organization,* in terms of efficiency, effectiveness, and health. In OD, standards of performance are not imposed upon the manager and his organization — rather, they arise from them. Yet these standards must reflect a concern for the total enterprise—for the welfare of its people as individuals and as groups as well as the welfare of the enterprise. Together, specific levels of efficiency, effectiveness, and health constitute a measure of total concern and commitment. This total system orientation and attendant focus on the individual and the organization set OD apart from traditional developmental approaches.

OD is not executive and/or management development revisited. Past experience is a ready reference for evaluating new events. Not surprisingly, many managers have looked on the new field of OD in the light of the more familiar programs of executive or management development and concluded that they are one and the same, "only the names have been changed." Such a perspective is mistaken and misleading. There are some historical antecedents of OD in executive and management development programs, from which OD borrows some techniques, but OD is far more than a remodeled, updated executive or management development program. It differs in purpose, in the problems it focuses on, and in processes. A discussion of these points will help managers evaluate OD on its own merits, unprejudiced by an association with executive and management development.

The purpose of executive and management development programs is to improve the general effectiveness of managers, in the belief that such improvements will enhance organizational effectiveness. The purpose of OD is to improve *overall* organizational efficiency, effectiveness, and health, not just the performance of a single organizational component. The aims of OD are clearly more comprehensive than are those of management development programs.

This same difference can be seen in the problems typically addressed by the two approaches. Executive and management development programs are typically used to rectify specific managerial deficiencies in knowledge or skills. For example, managers may need to know new company philosophy, policy, or procedures. They may need improvement in planning, coordinating, evaluating, and/or reporting the efforts of their units. Whether as orientation programs, career development patterns, or refresher courses, development programs focus on specific problems of managerial knowledge and skills acquisition.

OD programs, on the other hand, focus on problems related to organizational efficiency, effectiveness, and health. These may or may not include problems of managerial knowledge and skills needs. Typical problems addressed by OD include adaptation to management change, interorganizational conflict, lack of commitment to organizational objectives throughout the workforce, inefficient organizational structure, turnover, and lack of teamwork. Any problem which affects organizational performance can be addressed by OD. Only problems which evolve from the knowledge and/or skills deficiencies of managers can be addressed by development programs. This difference in scope is reflected in the processes used in each type of program.

Management development programs rely primarily upon traditional teaching techniques—courses, conferences, books and articles, and specialized training "packages" (such as PERT or MBO). In OD learning is experiential—on the job. Members of the organization (again, not just managers) learn while solving problems and solve problems while learning. The specific process employed is determined by diagnosis of the organization's needs. It may be data feedback, process consultation, team building, techno-structural change, or any one of a number of available OD strategies (Chapter 4 gives a complete listing). One way of expressing the difference in processes is to say that management development is done *to* managers *for* the organization. OD is done *by* the organization *with* and *for* all its members.

There are other differences between OD and management development programs in terms of time, transferability, and responsibility for design. Management development programs are of short duration. Their design is the responsibility of the trainer/teacher. Transfer of learning from the program back to the work setting is often a serious problem for the manager. OD is of longer duration. Responsibility for program design rests with the manager and the organization. The transfer problem is eliminated because the working and learning environments are one and the same under OD programs.

These differences between OD and executive development programs are summarized in Figure 1. It should be clear that OD is not a remodeled, updated version of management development. Managers should examine and evaluate OD on its own merits, not by mistaken association with its predecessors. There are fundamental differences in purpose, problem focus, and process which make OD a new and unique managerial phenomenon.

OD is a normative process of addressing the questions: "Where are we?" "Where do we want to be?" "How do we get from where we are to where we want to be?" This process is undertaken by members of the organization using a variety of techniques, often in collaboration with a behavioral science consultant.

Managers and students of management have long sought value-free universals that are applicable to their trade. This search for neutral "tools" which can be applied as managerial means to meet the ends of any organization, whatever its purposes, has led down many paths, all dead ends. Yet the search continues.

Many have advocated OD as a value-free technique adaptable to any organization. Too late, those who have initiated OD efforts have found them having a profound impact on the values of the organization. These managers have discovered OD to be value-laden, not value-free. The various approaches to

Figure 1. Organization development vs. management development.

	OD	MD
Purpose	To improve overall organizational performance	To improve managers' knowledge and skills
Problem-Focus	Any impediment to optimum organizational performance, such as: Managers' knowledge and skills Interorganizational conflict Lack of commitment Teamwork	Managers' knowledge and skills deficiencies: Company philosophy, policy, procedure Planning, coordinating, evaluating, reporting skills
Processes	Experiential learning, learning while solving problems and solving problems while learning through such means as: Data feedback Process consultation Team building Techno-structural change	Traditional teaching techniques: Courses, conferences Specialized training "packages" (PERT, MBO)
Responsibility for Program	The manager and his organization	The teacher or trainer
Time	Long duration, "real time"	Short, intense, "batch time"
Transfer of Learning	No difficulty	A major problem

OD reflect varying views on what is important in organizations, what is valued. An OD program cannot avoid influencing organizational philosophy, purposes, and processes. As managers choose from alternative approaches, they make choices between alternative values.

Informed choices about OD begin with acknowledging OD as a normative, value-laden process. Managers must, first, begin to appreciate OD as an inherently normative process. Second, managers must understand the underlying values and potential impact of alternative approaches to OD so that they will be better informed about OD choices for their organizations. The first two questions of OD may be viewed as determining the current state of operations or level of performance (Where are we?) and the desired state (Where do we want to be?). These questions and their answers constitute the *diagnostic phase* of any OD effort. The second general phase generates appropriate means for approaching the desired state (How do we get there?) and implements those means. This is typically termed the *intervention phase.* Every OD program has both diagnostic and intervention phases and is discussed in such terms in the literature. It may be more meaningful to managers to think of these phases in terms of the operational questions addressed.

Considerable emphasis should be placed upon the "we" in the operational questions above. OD is undertaken by members of the organization. In its programs, those who are responsible for the organization are responsible for developing the organization. When the problems are defined, the participants are identified. OD is not something done *to* the organization, it is something done *by* the organization. The organization may work collaboratively with an external or internal consultant, but at all times responsibility for development lies with the organization and its members, and, most importantly, with its managers.

The consultant's role in OD is to aid managers and members in identifying their needs and resources for developing the capabilities of the organization. In this role, the consultant relies upon his knowledge of management and behavioral science to bring what is known about individuals and organizations to bear upon the problems of individuals and organizations.

Finally, OD is a variety of techniques. It should be clear from this definition that there are many activities which may properly be called OD. These many activities, techniques, and strategies are here termed *approaches* to OD. The many approaches have in common the core properties of OD identified here, but they differ dramatically in the ways they make these properties operational in organizations.

These differences in approaches have important implications for managers as they consider OD choices for their organizations. Nothing so misleads managers as the many misconceptions which would have them believe that only one approach is OD. The most popular of these misconceptions is corrected below.

OD is not sensitivity training in organizations. Sensitivity training is but one of many approaches to OD. To define the field in terms of this particular approach is to insure that OD will be rejected by many, if not most, managers. No single definition of OD is more misleading. As a description of what OD is, it is overly restrictive and, therefore, inaccurate. As a prescription of what OD ought to be, it is organizationally naive.

It is all the more regrettable that this misconception has been widely held by many managers and others who have not had firsthand familiarity with OD. Managers who accept this definition as valid reject OD out of hand, and rightfully so, for they are quick to see its inappropriateness in many organizational contexts.

Managers readily understand that not all organizations are ready for T-groups and suspect that not all organizational problems can be resolved via sensitivity training. Not every organization is an appropriate host for the laboratory approach to change. The history, traditions, norms, values, and employees of many organizations are not receptive to the values and methods of laboratory training, as this approach is also known.

Moreover, not all organizational problems are amenable to solution via sensitivity training. Indeed, the approach can aggravate some problems. For example, considerable question currently exists about the applicability of T-groups to organizational problems of a political, structural, procedural, or technical nature. In some cases, T-groups have intensified existing organizational problems or created new ones. This has occurred most frequently when T-groups have gone deeper into people's personal lives and their interrelationships than the organization desires or is necessary, as, for example, when T-group methods of interpersonal encounter are used to solve a task or procedural problem.

Sensitivity training is one approach to OD, but it only one. It has all the properties common to all approaches to OD, and although there are some organizations and some organizational problems for which sensitivity training may be the best approach, there are many others for which it is not the best. To define the entire field of OD in terms of this single, controversial approach is to misinform and mislead managers and provoke their rejection of the opportunity OD can offer.

The following list is a summary of the points that have been made about the real meanings and the misconceptions of OD.

OD Is	*OD Is Not*
A conscious, planned process.	Any planned organizational change.
Concerned with developing the capabilities of an organization to attain and sustain optimum performance.	Executive or management development.
Measured by efficiency, effectiveness, *and* health.	Measured exclusively by either efficiency, effectiveness, *or* health.

OD Is	*OD Is Not*
A normative process of addressing the questions, "Where are we? Where do we want to be? How do we get there?" Done *by* organizations and their members.	Done *to* organizations and their members.
A variety of approaches.	Sensitivity training in organizations.

ILLUSTRATING THE DEFINITION

One remaining perspective on the definition of OD can contribute further to managers' comprehension of the field: case illustrations of the places, problems, purposes, and processes of OD. Such accounts bring to life otherwise abstract concepts by defining OD in the context of real managerial experiences. The cases introduced at the beginning of this chapter are continued here to provide an experiential backdrop for the definition of OD.

Case I Continued

Mike Mahlen's immediate problem was how to put a stop to the excessive turnover (150 percent annually) that was eroding his company's efficiency and effectiveness. Mike suspected, on the basis of his experience, that the turnover was symptomatic of broader problems. He felt that an OD program would bring those problems to the surface and begin to resolve them.

The consultant Mahlen contracted with began his diagnosis of the situation by attempting to discover where within the organization the problem was. He asked former employees, departing employees, and continuing employees and supervisors, "Why do people leave Mahlen's Maintenance?" Three reasons outnumbered all others. In order of frequency, they were: too much supervision ("The job is so simple, but they never let you alone to do it!"), no advancement in position or pay ("I would have been doing the same thing, earning the same money, whether I worked there six days, six months, or six years!"), and working conditions, particularly the lack of interaction with others ("I just got sick and tired of being by myself in that big building for eight hours every night.").

The consultant, following a standard survey feedback OD plan (described in Chapter 5), gave the results to Mahlen and his supervisory staff. He presented Mahlen with the choice of acting or not acting upon the data. In effect, the consultant asked management, "Where do you want to be?" Mahlen was prepared to do whatever was necessary to reduce turnover, with the exception of initiating pay increases, which he felt would weaken the financial position of the company. He also excluded widespread promotions, which would necessitate pay increases. In short, where Mahlen's Maintenance wanted to be was at a point where it had a stable workforce, and it wanted to get there without resorting to salary increases or promotions leading to salary increases.

The consultant pointed out the obvious, that without promotions or increases it would not be possible to retain employees dissatisfied with the company's promotion and pay policies. Several alternatives remained for redressing the conditions that promoted turnover. Each of these alternatives, like all OD interventions, had potential consequences for the total organization. The alternatives were presented to Mahlen, who discussed them with his maintenance supervisors.

The alternative interventions were mostly of a sociotechnical character, dealing with the structure of tasks and social relationships in the work environment. In outline, they were:

1. Decreasing direct supervision through
   (a) fewer supervisors
   (b) more independent workers with increased responsibility
   (c) more workers, reducing the supervisor/employee ratio.
2. Training supervisors to improve supervisory skills.
3. Increasing social interaction through
   (a) larger number of men assigned to one job
   (b) more shift meetings
   (c) transporting of men to and from jobs from a central location (main office).

Mahlen and his supervisors decided that their initial OD efforts would be to reduce the number of employees under direct supervision. A list of the most responsible employees was made, and the consultant met with this group to explain the overall plan and its purpose to them. They were then given assignments in which they were relatively independent of supervision. Over a period of six months *none* of the 20 employees so assigned left Mahlen Maintenance. Among other employees, however, turnover remained high.

As a result of the initial OD efforts and its effects, Mahlen established three categories and corresponding work assignments – supervised, semisupervised, unsupervised. A brief course was presented to acquaint supervisors with the skills needed in supervising each category. Over the next six-month period, turnover in Mahlen Maintenance was only 31 percent. Efficiency and effectiveness showed small but significant improvement over the same period.

Mahlen, still reluctant to deal with salaries and promotions, continues to explore alternative OD interventions for increasing social interaction and further reducing turnover. Everyone concerned considers the OD program a great success.

Case 2 Continued

Bud Paul's problem as director of the recreation division of a northwestern corporation was one of cooperation and commitment. The retention of a number of owner-managers of small facilities acquired by the corporation left Paul with a managerial core which he felt to be uncooperative and only marginally concerned with corporate goals. Bud Paul wanted the managers in his division to behave as a team. Frustrated in his own indirect and direct attempts to change their behavior, and unable to replace them, he contacted an OD consultant as a last resort.

The consultant's initial efforts focused on assessing the division's actual status. Did managers enforce corporate policies? Were managers committed to corporate goals? Interviews with different divisional managers supported Paul's perception. Most of them enforced only corporate policies consistent with policies they had pursued when they were owners. The managers admitted to having little real concern for corporate goals and in many instances little real knowledge of what the goals were.

The managers' reasons for their own behavior were very suggestive of where they wanted the corporate organization to be, which started the consultant on the second half of his diagnosis. The divisional managers felt very little commitment to corporate, or even divisional, goals because they had no voice in setting the goals. The managers' attitudes toward compliance with and enforcement of company policies were stated pretty strongly, too. Many of the policies were not consistent with conditions and client needs at individual facilities, yet they were to apply to all. The managers argued that different facilities required different policies, and if the corporation would not recognize this need, the managers would simply enforce only those policies which they felt suited their particular facility. In short, the managers were not a team, and while they saw some advantages in cooperative efforts, they saw no need to be a team under Bud Paul's rules.

The consultant communicated his findings to corporate headquarters, to Bud Paul, and to the managers. He further recommended that these three groups be brought together to clarify the issues and begin to develop action steps. All parties agreed—the managers perhaps reluctantly—and a standard team building OD intervention (explained in Chapter 5) was initiated.

At the first two-day meeting, each group was asked to rank by priority the major problems they experienced in the working relationship with each of the other two groups. These lists were then compiled and used to structure the agenda for the remainder of the first meeting and for subsequent meetings. It was decided that the first meeting would center on corporate goals—the development of goals, the communication of goals, and the commitment to goals by managers.

The meeting proved to be volatile. Corporate representatives explained the structure for developing corporate goals and the goals themselves. Bud Paul spoke of his attempts to communicate the corporate goals to the managers in his division. The managers aggressively attacked both the process and the product. The OD consultant acted as a facilitator, helping to make sure all views were not only aired but listened to. To ensure that criticism was heard openly and without defensiveness, he urged that it be presented in objective and constructive ways. By the end of the first day, what had begun as an adversary relationship was beginning to develop into a complementary relationship. Each of the three groups had become more receptive and more responsive to the others.

Building on the first day's work, the next day the participants drew up a consensus list of specific problems concerning corporate goals. The group then divided into three heterogeneous teams to create steps for solving problems. Work within these teams further enhanced the cooperative climate that was emerging. As a final step, the total group met to select from among the alternative problem-solving actions those which seemed most promising. Each individual accepted an assignment to be completed by the next meeting. It was agreed that corporate policies and the managers' responsibility would be the subject of the next team meeting.

The total history of Bud Paul's team is too lengthy to recount here (their method itself is covered in Chapter 5). It is enough to say that the OD effort generated results which were immediately apparent and positive to the corporation, to Bud Paul, and to the managers. So successful was this effort that teams and team building are now an integral part of every division of the corporation.

Case 3 Continued

The problems of Pete Kowalski were unlike those of either Mike Mahlen or Bud Paul, but they were no less amenable to the OD approach. Pete's problems were the problems of prosperity. Faced with demands for expansion of equipment, employees, and managerial and organizational skill over the next five years, Pete wanted his company to begin to plan now. Pete called upon an OD consultant to assist in the planning effort.

From diagnosis of where Kowalski's company was and where it wanted to be, the central problem which emerged was how to match organizational growth with personal growth. Another way of stating the problem was Pete's observation, "I'm afraid my company is going to outgrow my people." In specific terms, the OD effort had to deal with turning specialists into generalists, making people managers out of product managers, institutionalizing personal learning and growth, and keeping the organization's structure manageable.

Against this broad background the consultant sought to identify the personal plans of Pete's employees over the next five years. How did they view the growth of their job? their own growth? the jobs and growth of their peers? For many of Pete's people it was the first time they had seriously considered such questions.

From these data, personal development plans were plotted. An individual's personal development plan described his or her projected progress in the organization over the next five years. The plans were developed in peer groups working with the consultant. Programs were initiated to meet the needs indicated by the personal development plans and the organizational growth plans. Some employees were sent outside the organization for experience. Many packaged educational programs were purchased and brought into the organization for the benefit of all. Still other programs were designed inside the organization to meet developmental needs peculiar to the company.

This OD effort in Kowalski's plant does not fall easily into one category or another. It borrowed from many, using packaged programs, sociotechnical interventions, and laboratory training in an eclectic effort to meet the existing needs. Such eclecticism is perhaps more characteristic of OD than the "pure" strategies illustrated in the other two cases.

Shortly after the OD effort was well under way, design difficulties caused Kowalski's largest customer to renege on its contract. Boom nearly turned to bust. It is testimony to the success of the OD program that it was not set aside—pursuit was slowed, but progress continued. The excitement of planning for personal development *with* the organization kept all personnel on hand through some very lean pay periods. They believed that continued pursuit of their development as planned would ultimately renew the development of the organization, and today their belief appears to be realized.

ONCE AGAIN—WHAT IS OD?

These three cases accurately reflect much of what is going on with OD in management today. OD is being called upon by companies of all sizes, at various points in their individual histories, to meet problems of every description and order. OD answers that call with a simple operational framework: Where are we? Where do we want to be? How do we get there from here? Underlying the apparent simplicity of OD are complex properties of purpose and values, and an infinite array of processes. These are critical to managers' choices about OD and belie many popularly held misconceptions. The difference between what OD is and is not is often, for managers, the difference between the effective use and the abuse of OD.

This chapter's attention to the definition of OD, the explanation of its central properties, the exposure of misconceptions, and the illustration of its meaning in managerial contexts has all been intended to clarify OD for managers. Additional understanding of what OD is comes from some knowledge of what OD was—thus Chapter 2 presents a brief history of OD for managers.

The History of OD

It has been commonplace among operating managers to criticize emergent developments in management as mere academic inventions serving only the needs of those who invent them. In many instances such criticism from the field is accurate. But not in the case of OD. What is little known or recognized is that the origins of OD lie, not in the inventive imaginations of academics and consultants, but instead in the experiences and needs of operating managers. A knowledge of key developments in the history of OD will enhance managers' understanding of the field.

THE IDEA OF OD

OD as a body of theory and practice is relatively new. In many respects it is still emerging and taking form. The formal history of OD dates only from 1957–1958. The antecedents of OD, however, can be traced directly to post-World War II organizational needs and practices.

During World War II and in the immediate postwar years, all organizations, public and private, faced critical manpower and resource shortages. As managers experienced these shortages, they were stimulated to search for effective means for getting the maximum possible use out of existing individual and organizational resources. At times managers were joined in this search by social scientists. Two methods for stretching scarce personnel and production resources became prominent in business, industry, and government. One method, personnel training, was expected to provide the needed managerial manpower for organizations. A second method, long-range organizational planning, was relied upon to maximize utilization of production resources.

It is important to note that this emphasis on personnel training and long-range organizational planning was contemporaneous but not cooperative. The development of individuals and the development of organizations were considered as separate and distinct activities and pursued as such. There were two avenues toward maximizing individual and organizational resources, not one.

This obvious paradox—the development of individuals in organizations as a concern and activity apart from the development of organizations and vice versa—did not go unnoticed by those managers concerned with maximizing both individual and organizational effectiveness. In 1945 Leland P. Bradford, who was responsible for training within the many units which comprised the Federal Security Agency, condemned the practice, in public and private organizations alike, of employing piecemeal efforts to improve one or another part of the organization without regard for the whole. As an alternative, Bradford introduced a new concept, training as an integrated managerial program of individual *and* organizational growth.[1]

Bradford's perspective, unique in its time among training personnel, was nonetheless embraced by operating managers as a view consistent with their experiences. Many managers realized that, however narrow the content of a training program, the consequences of training affected the entire organization. They also understood that continued development could not be achieved through sole concentration upon improvement of either individuals or organizations to the neglect of the other. Managers, like Bradford, looked for management techniques that would identify problems, develop solutions, uncover further problems, and develop further solutions. Managers sought a way of addressing these issues that would be diagnostic and therapeutic for both individuals and the organization as a whole.

Management techniques that were developmental for individuals and the organization, the vision held by Bradford and the need experienced by managers, were not possible without prior changes in training methods. In 1945, few training programs were designed or implemented as diagnostic and therapeutic for the individual or for the organization. Training was a poorly used management tool commonly employed as a reactive measure to meet situational crises as they arose, rather than as an activity integral to a planned program for organizational growth. Training methods in vogue at the time were correspondingly narrow in their content and shortsighted in their consequences. Most programs were little more than training in basic job skills. The emergence of an integrated managerial program of individual and organizational growth was dependent upon the prior development of new training methods and new models for the application of those methods within organizations.

[1] Leland P. Bradford, "Resistance to Re-Education in Government Administration," *Journal of Social Issues,* March 1945, p. 38.

THE CONTRIBUTION OF TRAINING TO OD

Of the many new training methods which emerged in the postwar years, the one to have the most profound impact upon the development of OD was the "basic skill training group." This was later shortened to its popular form, "T-group," also known as "laboratory training" and "sensitivity training." Today laboratory training is but one of many approaches to OD and bears little resemblance to its earlier forms. However, in 1946 the invention of the laboratory method constituted the breakthrough in traditional training that provided an important impetus for the development of OD. Simply expressed, the laboratory method involved group participants receiving feedback about their own behavior in the group and using that feedback as data for learning about themselves and others. The group acted as a laboratory in which participants generated data for their own learning much as a scientist might generate data in a research laboratory.

Early experiments with the laboratory method led to two important conclusions which affected the emergence of OD. First, it was observed that giving group participants feedback about their interactions in the group provided rich personal learning experiences. The laboratory method was thus quickly identified as a new and exciting approach to individual training and education. The second major conclusion was that the process of group building and the learning derived from the laboratory method were, not only meaningful to individuals while they were in the laboratory setting, but also relevant and appropriate to back-at-the-office organizational situations. These early observations on the inherent and applied value of the laboratory method shaped its utilization in organizational training programs for nearly a decade. OD emerged in part as an extension of and in part as a reaction to this usage.

Encouraged by their early successes, proponents of the laboratory method sought and won support for further programs and experiments. The National Training Laboratory in Group Development (later shortened to National Training Laboratory and popularly known as NTL) was established in 1949 as a center for the study and use of the laboratory method as a training tool and learning experience. NTL sponsored many experiments with the laboratory method inside and outside of organizations. These experiments led to changes.

The name change itself—from basic skill training groups to T-groups and sensitivity groups—reflected the shift in emphasis from group skills training to interpersonal and intrapersonal learning. The shift was from learning about the self in relation to others to learning about the self. The focus on experimentation and the form of experiments under the laboratory method diverted the attention of leaders in the training field from the need for corresponding changes in the application of this method within organizations. These corresponding changes were necessary to realize training as a planned managerial program of individual and organizational growth. It was not until the late 1950s, almost a decade after the inception of the laboratory method, that NTL and its membership became active in the application of this method within planned organizational programs of growth and development.

This is not to say that no efforts were made to utilize the laboratory method in organizational training programs. Many such attempts were made in the late 1940s and particularly the early 1950s as managers sought to take advantage of this innovation in training. Many managers believed that the new methods would enrich both individuals and the organization. The programs commonly took the name of "human relations training" or "group dynamics." Typically, top- and middle-level managers left their organizations to receive training at an off-site retreat for periods of anywhere from three days to two weeks. There they gathered in groups to examine their own ideas and attitudes on supervision and to explore new ones. Working in groups, they acquired new group skills so that they might apply their new attitudes on the job. The trained managers were then returned to the work site to put into practice their newly acquired skills and attitudes.

Managers exposed to human relations or group dynamics training programs often had a hard time reentering the organization and experienced even more difficulty in attempting to implement their new learning effectively. Research findings indicated what several participating managers had already expected— after a short time back on the job, the trained managers and supervisors were less effective than their colleagues who had not received training.

This post-training decline in managerial effectiveness reflected the differences between what the managers learned in training and what was expected of them in their jobs. The new attitudes and skills acquired through human relations and group dynamics training were often at odds with the behavior expected of managers by their subordinates, peers, and superiors. Managers found themselves either opposing their supervisors or resuming practices they now thought to be less effective than those they had learned in training programs. This conflict between individual development and the demands of the organization came to be viewed by many as the "top management dilemma."

On recognizing this dilemma, participating managers and trainers alike concluded that effective training programs should be concerned with the organizational setting as well as with individual managerial behavior. Effective change processes needed to consider both the forces within an individual and the forces in the organizational situation surrounding the individual, so that new individual behavior would be rewarded and encouraged with organizational support.

Several designs were developed and implemented with this balance in mind. The Institute of Industrial Relations at the University of California, Los Angeles encouraged the use of vertically structured training groups, representing all levels of a working unit, in an effort to deal with individual managers within their organizational units. The Survey Research Center at the University of Michigan developed the "survey-feedback" technique for relating data from individuals to the work group. The Research Center for Group Dynamics, also at the University of Michigan, formulated a series of steps for diagnosing, planning, and acting on organizational change.

These and numerous other training designs and programs attempted to maximize the effectiveness of organizational training activities by integrating the individual and organizational emphases. In so doing they contributed to the further development of OD. These designs were largely experimental, and though they later became distinct approaches to OD, they did not have a great impact at the time of their inception.

One program which significantly affected organizational activities was developed by the Training Division of the California State Personnel Board in 1954. The program is also important because it was the first to articulate and implement a program of "organization development." In 1954 the Training Division, acting under Neely D. Gardner, committed itself to two major goals: to develop an organizational climate which not only permitted training but also facilitated use of the results of that training in the organization and to develop the concept of training as an integral part of the organization's activity.[2]

The Training Division viewed its program as organization development, giving attention to both individual and organizational issues. For example, managers were given practice in interpersonal management skills, which boosted their confidence and their ability to improve the effectiveness of work relationships. At the organizational level, the managers' use of these skills was supported and encouraged, first, by training a corps of managers with the same skills so that they might support one another; second, by developing a communications network to facilitate manager-employee interactions; and, third, by using interpersonal skills and employee development processes to discover and solve organizational problems. Individual improvement and organizational improvement were seen as necessary complements to one another.

Although the underlying idea and the name are the same, the organization development program developed by the California State Personnel Board in 1954 bears only slight resemblance to current OD efforts. The critical differ-

[2]Neely D. Gardner, "Training as a Framework for Action," *Public Personnel Review,* January 1957, pp. 39–44.

ence is one of emphasis. While the Training Division's program was a major move toward the balanced pursuit of individual and organizational development that managers and researchers agreed was needed, its primary emphasis was on individual training to alter attitudes and behavior. The organizational context was acknowledged as important, and an attempt was made to relate training to key organizational elements, but this emphasis was decidedly secondary to the focus on improving individuals' skills.

DEPARTMENTS OF ORGANIZATION DEVELOPMENT

In business and industry, further progress toward equal emphasis on the individual and the organization was contemporaneous with the training programs described above. It is interesting that these developments also occurred under the banner of "organization development." However, here the term generally referred to activities only remotely related to training.

During World War II the government required businesses and industry to furnish detailed manning tables and job descriptions to prevent the hoarding of scarce skilled personnel. After the war the shortage of managerial personnel continued as the job mix altered. Long-range planning for organizational personnel needs was initially only an extension of these government requirements. It consisted primarily of job evaluation and rationalization of organization structure using boxes and charts. Soon, long-range analysis of these needs was recognized as an important staff function. Departments of organization, departments of organization planning, and departments of organization development were created. They were usually separate from traditional training programs, which were under personnel departments. Departments of organization development were kept separate because they called for organization analysis skills rather than mere job training.

These departments of organization development proliferated in the 1950s. Their specific activities varied greatly from firm to firm, but three general levels could be identified. At the first level, some departments focused on problems of the total corporation and worked toward their solution by changing the organization's structure, the attitudes and behavior of the people, and the communication and decision-making processes. Today such a perspective on the organization and its problems is often called a "total systems approach." On the second level, other departments of organization development approached corporate problems solely through modifications and changes in the organization's structure. At the third level, still others employed the structural approach in working with problems of the operational units of the firm.

By far most departments of organization development fell within the second level. These engaged in such activities as developing the long-range organization plan, writing corporate and organization policy manuals, and preparing organization studies and audits. While some attention was given to individuals through executive career development plans, it was secondary to the attention given organizational structure. In these departments the balance between individual and organizational needs leaned toward the organization, in contrast to the emphasis on the individual noted in the Training Division program.

The Training Division organization development program and the corporate departments of organization development both attempted to integrate, in idea and in practice, individual *and* organizational diagnosis and change. In so doing, these programs addressed the needs of managers and departed radically from traditional managerial concepts of training and organizational planning. They were built from and on the experiences of managers. Both were important steps in evolving the present conceptions and practices of OD. This evolution culminated in 1957 in the Esso Standard Oil Company organization development program, which combined diagnosis and change for both individuals and the organization in what is generally regarded as the first OD program.[3]

THE ESSO OD EFFORT

The program developed and implemented at Esso Standard Oil during 1957–1958 was certainly not the first organizational change effort. Nor was Esso's the only program of organizational change in progress in the 1950s. It was but one of many. Yet the Esso program is pivotal in the history of OD for its definition, in both concept and form, of the essential elements of OD. The Esso OD program's requirements for starting and carrying through an organization development program stated its conceptual base. These requirements were, first a framework in which needs can be diagnosed through individuals and the organization by asking "Where are we?" and "Where do we want to be?" and, second, a theory of change for developing procedures for moving from the former to the latter, answering the question "How do we get from where we are to where we want to be?"

In practice, the program at Esso built on this base with balanced emphasis on individuals and the organization. Both were viewed as equally important and inherently interrelated in both diagnostic and change activities. For

[3] *An Action Research Program for Organization Improvement,* Esso Research Division (Ann Arbor, Mich.: Foundation for Research on Human Behavior, 1960).

example, some personal developmental needs were identified and looked upon as symptomatic of organizational conditions, and vice versa. Such conditions often were remedied through training programs designed to aid or alter individual behavior, with concurrent organizational changes to facilitate and support the new behavior. The Esso program defined OD as an important new field of theory and practice for behavioral scientists and operating managers.

OD MADE PUBLIC

Largely through the efforts of the Foundation for Research on Human Behavior, the Esso program, and with it the theory and practice of OD, was brought to the attention of a larger audience concerned with organizational change. The foundation, a nonprofit privately funded organization in Ann Arbor, Michigan, had two primary purposes. First, it provided a means for interested companies to pool research funds for more effective basic research on organizational effectiveness, economic behavior, and public communication. Second, it brought together businessmen and social scientists to plan needed research and to discuss applications of research findings to practical business problems. The foundation followed closely the OD effort of Esso, one of its corporate sponsors.

In the spring of 1959 the foundation held two seminars on organizational change to review existing knowledge in the area and to draw attention to the need for increased research. Participants included those who had been or who were responsible for changes in business organizations and government agencies, university researchers who had studied organizational change, and academics and practicing managers who anticipated assuming major roles in organizational change in the future.

The seminars, through reports on research and case studies, reached two conclusions that provided the springboard for the takeoff of OD in the 1960s. First, OD's contribution and relevance to organizational efficiency, effectiveness, and health was affirmed by managers and researchers alike. Second, the importance of continued investment of effort and funds in OD was underscored. These conclusions summarized one phase in OD's evolution and began another. The foundation's program presented to academic, business, and government communities the considerable work in progress in OD, summarizing 15 years of development. The program also demonstrated OD's proven and potential contributions to individual and organizational efficiency and effectiveness. This instigated a full decade of growth and maturation of the field.

Reviewing this history, the strong influence of operating managers' needs and experiences upon OD is evident. OD was initially conceived as a means of addressing individual and organizational needs. Various experimental programs and procedures were evaluated against the experiences of participating managers. Many of these experimental forms reappeared as separate approaches to OD. This evolutionary cycle—expressed need, experimentation, experience, and evaluation—culminated in the Esso OD effort. The success and visibility of that effort spawned the tremendous surge of interest and involvement in OD programs in the 1960s.

Knowledge of the history of OD helps to put present experiences into perspective. It is an important complement to managers' understanding of what OD is. But knowing what OD is and where it comes from only begins to answer operating managers' many questions. They also want and need to know how specific approaches to OD will affect them and their organizations. To make appropriate choices, they need a framework for comparing alternative approaches. Such a comparative framework for managers is presented in Chapter 3.

Dimensions of Organization Development

Managers do many things and play many roles. One recent listing claims that there are ten primary types of managerial activities—three interpersonal, three informational, and four decisional. In his interpersonal roles, the manager acts as a *figurehead*—the formal representative of his organization—as a *liaison* officer for managers and others outside his own organization, and as the *leader* of his organization, with all that may imply. In his informational activities, he is a *monitor* receiving and collecting information, a *disseminator* diffusing this information through his organization, and a *spokesman* transmitting organizational information into the environment. In his role as decision maker, he is an *entrepreneur* who initiates change, a *disturbance handler* who resolves conflict when the organization is threatened, a *resource allocator* who decides where the organization will spend its efforts, and a *negotiator* on behalf of the organization.[1]

At times these many roles and activities are complementary, but more often they are competing and conflicting. The successful manager very quickly gains an appreciation of the *opportunity cost* of his own and his organization's time, of the benefits forgone by doing one thing instead of another. No matter what he is doing, the manager is constantly faced with what he might do instead and what he must yet do. Above all else, then, the manager makes choices, choices about his own and his organization's activities.

DIMENSIONS OF OD AND MANAGERIAL CHOICES

These choices managers make are governed by criteria reflecting their dominant concerns. Specific criteria vary from organization to organization and from manager to manager, but the basic managerial concerns remain constant.

---

[1] Henry Mintzberg, *The Nature of Managerial Work* (New York: Harper & Row, 1973).

For example, all managers are price conscious—the comparative cost of available alternatives is always a primary consideration. But cost is a relative measure, and what is one manager's bargain may be another's pure extravagance. What they share is a concern for price; what they differ on is the price they are willing to have their organizations pay.

In their consideration of choices in such functional areas as priorities, personnel, products, and promotion, managers are guided by such constant concerns as price, planning, power, personal relationships, pace, professional relationships, and performance.[2] These same concerns should guide managers as they consider alternative approaches to OD, which differ in their effects on managerial plans, power, personal relationships, and so on. Managers' first need is for a framework in which to examine these effects. They also need an elaboration and an evaluation of the effects. This chapter addresses the first of these needs, and Chapters 4 and 5 the latter two.

The following framework for evaluating alternative approaches to OD within the areas of their critical choice concerns gives managers a tool for understanding the full implications of these approaches for their organizations. Thus informed, they will be able to make appropriate OD choices.

The Nature of the Plan

A major managerial role is that of resource allocator. It is the manager who decides where and how the organization will spend its efforts—he plans for his organization. The nature of planning differs from one organization to the next, reflecting the different styles of their managers. Manager A prefers to specify proposed organizational activity in minute detail, step by step. Manager B, planning for the same outcome, only outlines the objectives and allows specific steps to emerge as they will. Despite their different styles, both managers plan to the degree appropriate for their own organization.

The degree of managerial planning is an important consideration in differentiating between approaches to OD characterized by different degrees of planning. For example, some approaches to OD pursue development through a series of detailed, tightly scheduled steps: "At the third meeting the Planning Committee will set objectives and develop a method for collecting data. Time allotted, 2–4 hours." Other approaches are more free-form: "The manager and his staff will go off for 2 or 3 days to work on general guidelines for the program."

---

[2] Larry Greiner, "Patterns of Organizational Change," *Harvard Business Review,* May–June 1967, pp. 119–130. Greiner was among the first to discuss organizational change approaches in terms of plan, power, personal relationships, and pace. The other dimensions are original to this author.

Obviously some managers will feel more comfortable with highly structured OD approaches. Others will prefer relatively unstructured approaches. The key point is that the nature of the plan within alternative OD approaches should be an important criterion in managers' choices about OD.

Three broad categories of plans provide a scale for scoring alternative approaches to OD. One extreme reflects attention to detail and timing of OD steps far in advance. This category of specific, scheduled plans is *structured*. At the opposite extreme are plans that emerge from the process in actual execution, without prior attention to specifics or to scheduling. Such free-form plans can be called *unstructured*.

Many managers pursue organizational activities after a fashion that is neither strictly structured nor unstructured. For these managers planning is an incremental process of setting long-range objectives, then matching short-range means to immediate conditions. Many approaches to OD reflect in their plans the same concern for short-range flexibility in pursuit of long-range goals. Such plans fall at the midpoint on a planning scale and can be categorized as *sequentially structured*. The resulting scale for weighing the degree of planning in alternative approaches to OD is outlined in Figure 2.

Figure 2. The nature of plans in OD approaches.

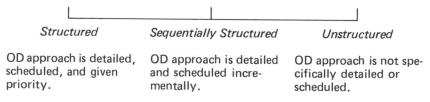

Structured	Sequentially Structured	Unstructured
OD approach is detailed, scheduled, and given priority.	OD approach is detailed and scheduled incrementally.	OD approach is not specifically detailed or scheduled.

It is important to note that this scale (as well as those following) suggests a means of assessing the properties of alternative approaches to OD. By scoring the various approaches (as described in Chapter 5), managers will gain the information necessary to make the comparative judgments critical to effective choice.

The Nature of Power

If one were to summarize in a single word the many roles that managers play, that word would most likely be *power*. Managers have power. Their many interpersonal, informational, and decisional roles give them the power to make decisions, the power to get things done.

Different managers wield their power differently, as best fits their needs and their organizations'. The uses of power can be differentiated through the

Continuum of Leadership Behavior (see Figure 3), a tool familiar to many managers.[3]

Figure 3. Continuum of leadership behavior.

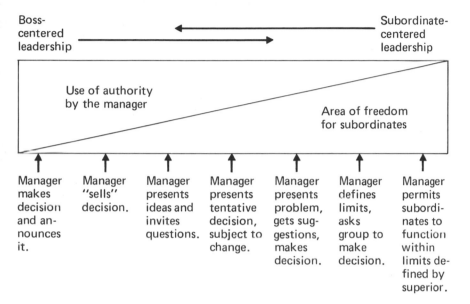

| Manager makes decision and announces it. | Manager "sells" decision. | Manager presents ideas and invites questions. | Manager presents tentative decision, subject to change. | Manager presents problem, gets suggestions, makes decision. | Manager defines limits, asks group to make decision. | Manager permits subordinates to function within limits defined by superior. |

At the heart of organizational power is the question "Who is making the decisions?" The continuum illustrates varying answers based on the balance of power between the manager and his subordinates. At one extreme, power rests entirely with the manager: He identifies a problem, generates and evaluates alternative solutions, then chooses a solution and announces it to his subordinates for implementation. Decisional power in this instance is solely the prerogative of the manager; at this end of the continuum, power is *unilateral.*

One alternative balance of organizational power offers a more even distribution of manager and subordinate input to decisions. The manager presents a tentative decision—or he simply presents the problem—gets subordinates' suggestions, then makes his decision. In either instance the decision is shared between the manager and his subordinates. There are, of course, other patterns based on more equitable distributions of decision power. All such pat-

---

[3] Robert Tannenbaum and Warren H. Schmidt, "How to Choose a Leadership Pattern," *Harvard Business Review,* March–April 1957, pp. 95–101.

terns involve subordinate participation in and acceptance of the manager's decision, patterns most simply described as *shared*.

At the other extreme of the continuum from unilateral are decision patterns reflecting power distributed in favor of subordinates. In these instances the manager may define the limits and ask subordinates to make a decision, or he may allow subordinates to make the decisions they deem appropriate. In either case ultimate responsibility for decisions still remains with the manager, who delegates to subordinates his power to decide. These organizational power patterns are obviously *delegated*.

In selecting a pattern for decisions, managers must be sensitive to their own needs, the needs of their subordinates, and the demands of specific decision situations. The distribution of power shifts as these needs and demands shift. Managers within the same organization may use their power in very different but equally effective ways as they respond to different needs.

Like organizations and managers, approaches to OD reflect different power patterns. Underlying each approach are implications for the distribution of power between the manager and his subordinates. At times these implications are quite obvious; team building, for example, is clearly intended to bring about equalization in the distribution of power. At other times the approaches' different implications for organizational power are not as clear. Taking another example, the intended effect of survey feedback OD on the distribution of power between a manager and his subordinates may not be at all clear to the manager. However, on implementation survey feedback OD tends to support unilateral distribution of power, since under its plan information is first reported to those at the top. The manager who has this knowledge about potential effects of survey feedback OD will be able to make an appropriate, informed decision regarding its use.

Knowledge of the delegation of power within alternative approaches to OD is critical to a manager's choice of the approach most appropriate for his organization. The power dimensions of approaches to OD can be scored on a relative scale using the unilateral, shared, and delegated qualifications shown in Figure 4.

Figure 4. The nature of power in OD approaches.

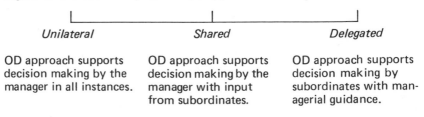

Unilateral	Shared	Delegated
OD approach supports decision making by the manager in all instances.	OD approach supports decision making by the manager with input from subordinates.	OD approach supports decision making by subordinates with managerial guidance.

The Nature of Personal Relationships

Perhaps the greatest variations in the behavior of managers are in the interpersonal roles they play. The figurehead, liaison, and leadership roles of the manager mirror the style he finds comfortable. For some managers that style brings them very close to all the people in their organization. There is, for them, no conflict between work relationships and personal relationships— indeed, they find them complementary. Employees are people, foremost, perhaps even intimate friends; the personal relationships they offer are among the rewards of management and are sought accordingly.

For another (probably larger) group of managers the organization is not a place to pursue personal relationships. These managers are more comfortable with a certain distance between themselves and their subordinates and take a relatively impersonal approach to their work.

Finally, there are managers who are comfortable with personal relationships in their work only to the extent that those relationships are defined by the work situation. They work intimately with subordinates, but they probably would not seek such intimacy if it were not demanded by the job.

Managers are, of course, not alone in their differing degrees of comfort with personal relationships in the organization. The same could be said of every member of the organization. Indeed, organizations and work groups might be characterized by the kinds of relationships which seem prevalent in them. Some organizations or work groups, notably small ones, have frequent and intense personal interaction between employees across work assignments and across levels, perhaps off the job as well. The nature of interpersonal relationships in these organizations is clearly very *personal*.

In other organizations interpersonal relationships may be confined to work, with no great frequency or intensity of personal interaction beyond that required by the structure of work. In such situations those who work together invest in their personal relationships with one another, and those who do not work together do not make that investment. These are best described as *personal-work* relationships.

Finally, in many organizations personal relationships are of little concern. Perhaps because of the nature and/or structure of the work, the personal style of the manager, or the personal styles of employees, some organizations show no investment in personal relationships. This is not to suggest that these organizations are less effective than others, only that they have a different style in interpersonal relationships which is relatively *impersonal*.

All approaches to OD affect, in one fashion or another, the nature of personal relationships in organizations, and every approach to OD makes implicit or explicit assumptions about the level of personal relationships within the organization. Knowledge of these assumptions is critical to a manager's choice of an approach that is consistent with the character of relations in his organization. In its implementation, every approach to OD can assume personal or impersonal overtones.

Nonetheless, it is possible to make general statements about the nature of personal relationships in any given approach to OD relative to other approaches. For example, during the diagnostic stage, a techno-structural approach may on the one hand be concerned with thorough discussion of the personal problems of workers and the implications for their work, or it may on the other hand merely take the form of an impersonal pen and paper survey questionnaire. It is fair to say, however, that relative to such approaches as laboratory training the techno-structural approach tends to be rather impersonal. The scale (Figure 5) for scoring the nature of personal relationships in approaches to OD reflects the three broad types.

Figure 5. The nature of personal relationships in OD approaches.

Impersonal	*Personal-Work*	*Personal*
OD approach does not consider personal relationships.	OD approach considers only personal relationships developed by the work situation.	OD approach considers personal relationships in and out of work.

The Nature of the Pace

A fourth criterion of major importance to managers choosing among alternative roles and activities is timing. An effective manager is not only one who is in the right place at the right time, but also one who does the right thing in the right place at the right time. In other words, he must have a sense of timing—he must be attuned to the pulse of his people and their tolerance for different tempos as well as to the tempo of action demanded by a situation.

Organizations develop characteristic paces. Some operate as if they were responding to a continual condition of crisis. From the manager on down, the work pace is hectic, even frenetic. Work is generated, completed, and regenerated in a fast and furious atmosphere of time scarcity. In these organizations, rightly or wrongly, "speed is king."

Other organizations reflect a measured pace: Work proceeds much more slowly from inception through completion. Time is not a scarce resource, but rather appears to exist in abundance. The pace is almost leisurely. In still other organizations work proceeds at an incrementally increasing pace. What starts out very slowly may quicken toward conclusion in a regulated fashion.

The manager must be sensitive to the pace of his people and their work, and he must select activities and play his own roles in ways which do not jar the organization out of a productive pace. The tempo of activity, or pace, is particularly important where initiating change is concerned, as it is in OD.

In some organizations, for some changes, the most effective approaches will be those which evolve slowly. Such approaches are properly *evolutionary*. In other organizations, or for other changes, a faster pace may be more appropriate, one which is *incremental*—it builds on itself. Finally, there are organizations and change circumstances in which the most *rapid* approach will be the most effective.

In choosing the pace of his activity, the manager must consider not only the timing tolerances of his people but also the inherent tempo of the activities themselves. He needs an appreciation of the pace of change in alternative approaches to OD. This can be gained by rating the pace of OD approaches on the scale in Figure 6.

Figure 6. The nature of pace in OD approaches.

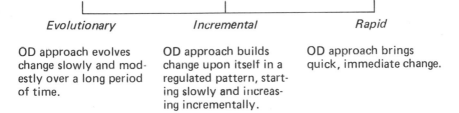

Evolutionary	Incremental	Rapid
OD approach evolves change slowly and modestly over a long period of time.	OD approach builds change upon itself in a regulated pattern, starting slowly and increasing incrementally.	OD approach brings quick, immediate change.

The Nature of the Price

Operating managers are well acquainted with cost as a critical concern. For many managers cost is a criterion outweighing all others. There is little need to emphasize the importance of cost in relation to OD. However, it is helpful to consider the character of costs managers must consider as they confront alternative approaches to OD.

The critical costs in considering OD are real costs and opportunity costs. Real costs are the monetary investments involved in initiating and supporting an OD effort: consultant fees, support services, and salaries paid for time involved in OD. In general, the more external skill is required for any given approach to OD, the greater will be the real costs of that approach, but consultant fees vary so greatly that this observation gives only an approximate yardstick.

Too often, cost considerations center solely on real costs, ignoring opportunity costs, which are the time and energy investment required of the organization. They amount to the benefits forgone by investing time and energy in OD instead of in another activity. For example, the costs of time and energy invested in a team building OD effort are determined in part by the benefits forfeited by not spending that same time and energy on inventory control or some other direct organizational task. In general, the greater the organizational participation or member involvement required by any given approach to OD, the greater will be its opportunity costs.

Real costs and opportunity costs together represent the *price* of any OD approach. Of the two cost components, opportunity costs are more important because they vary less within a given approach — that is, for any one approach to OD, managers can shop for lower real costs (especially consultant fees), but the opportunity costs will be relatively the same no matter which approach is chosen. Consultant fees for a three-day team building session may range from $100 per day to $750 or $1,000 per day, depending upon the consultant. Whatever the consultant's fee, however, the benefits forgone by involving a group of top managers in team building for three days, to the exclusion of their normal activities, will be relatively fixed, and probably quite high for most organizations. This, of course, sidesteps the premise that the more a consultant charges the better he is and the more he benefits the organization — as managers know, there is not necessarily a relationship between price and performance.

Real costs cannot be ignored, but it is the opportunity costs of an approach to OD which set the prices managers must consider as they make choices about OD. In determining the price of any approach to OD, its opportunity costs have to be established. In estimating opportunity costs it must be assumed that the time and energy invested in OD would be productively invested elsewhere if they were not given to OD. As a result, the expected benefits from the amount of time and energy invested elsewhere in the organization constitute the opportunity cost of OD.

Thus, approaches to OD requiring little member participation in time or energy have low opportunity costs and are therefore relatively *inexpensive.* Approaches to OD requiring extensive time and energy commitments have high opportunity costs and are comparatively *expensive.* If the investment required is between these two extremes, then the price of that approach is *moderate.* The relative prices of alternative approaches to OD can be assessed on a scale (Figure 7) similar to those used for other criteria.

The Nature of the Professional Relationship

Managerial concern about the effects of activity on the balance of organizational power extends outside as well as throughout the organization. Where managers find themselves relying on outside services, they are quick to raise

Figure 7. The nature of price in OD approaches.

Inexpensive	Moderate	Expensive
OD approach has variable real costs and low time and energy requirements resulting in low opportunity costs.	OD approach has variable real costs and moderate time and energy requirements resulting in moderate opportunity costs.	OD approach has variable real costs and high time and energy requirements resulting in high opportunity costs.

questions of control: "Who decides what is needed? How much? How will it be applied?" These questions define the *professional relationship* between the manager and the contractor consultant. This definition is essential to ensure the effectiveness of their joint efforts. Whether the consultant is an architect, accountant, lawyer, market analyst, or OD expert, there must be a clear understanding of what decisions are to be made by whom and how—the balance of power between the manager and the consultant must be established.

The kind of relationship which evolves between a manager and a consultant is a product of their preferred advisory styles. Certain consultancy models seem more natural to some disciplines than to other—legal advice is not sought or offered in the same manner as architectural plans would be. These tendencies notwithstanding, the working relationship and distribution of power between the manager and a consultant are primarily shaped by their preferences, rather than by the kinds of services involved.

There are three basic models in management consulting, each embracing a variety of specific styles and strategies. They are differentiated by the balance of power between the manager and the consultant, not by the kinds of problems they address, and they apply to all disciplines, not just to OD.

The oldest and most popular is the "medical" model, in which the relationship between the manager and the consultant is like that between a patient and his doctor. The patient hurts, so he calls the doctor and tells him where it hurts; the doctor examines the patient, asks probing questions, then gives a diagnosis and prescribes a cure. The medical model of management consulting follows this point by point: The manager hurts; he sees signs (turnover, low productivity, bad morale) that something is wrong, but he doesn't know what is wrong or how to put it right, so he calls in a consultant. The consultant examines the organization, asks probing questions, then renders a diagnosis and prescribes a cure.

In the medical model, power rests with the consultant (doctor). He decides which symptoms are acute and which are benign, what real illness has befallen the organization, and what remedies must be applied. He makes the decisions regarding the demand, design, and delivery of his knowledge and skills. The professional relationship between the manager and the consultant is decidedly *consultant-centered.*

In contrast to the consultant's position of power under the medical model, lack of power characterizes other consultant/manager relationships. For instance, in the "consumer" or "purchase" model, the manager is a buyer of consultant services. He defines his company's needs, determines what items or services will meet these needs, and shops for the desired services in the marketplace. In this model, the manager is the purchaser of consultant expertise just as a consumer is a purchaser of goods and services in a store or business.

Consumers are influenced by marketing attempts to create a need or to meet an existing need with a particular product or service. Managers are subject to similar influence, and their diagnosis of problems and determination of needs may be shaped, in part, by the very consultants they hire. This is a common result of consultants' presentations at managerial meetings and is the main reason consultants seek such opportunities. However, throughout the professional relationship between manager and consultant in the consumer model, it is the manager—the client—who dominates. He decides the demand, design, and delivery of the consultant's knowledge and skills. Here the professional relationship between the manager and the consultant is decidedly *client-centered.*

There are relationships in which the client and the consultant share responsibility. While they lack such ready labels as the medical or purchase model, relationships following this pattern of shared responsibility are equally effective, if not equally popular. Perhaps the "broker" model comes closest to naming this relationship. The client and the consultant act with mutual responsibility for diagnosing needs and for generating and choosing alternatives. The manager presents the consultant "broker" with his own assessment of the company's needs and resources, and the broker applies his special skills and knowledge to identify additional needs and resources. Together they make decisions on a course of action. Except for the manager's ultimate veto power, in such professional relationships effective power is weighted in favor of neither the client nor the consultant, but is in fact *dual.*

OD approaches include all three types of professional relationships between the manager and the consultant. These types, therefore, provide another measure of aid to managers in their selection of the approach most appropriate for their organization. (See Figure 8.)

The Nature of Performance Criteria

The final managerial measure of alternative approaches to OD considers how the performance of OD is assessed. A constant measure of any organi-

Figure 8. The nature of professional relationships in OD approaches.

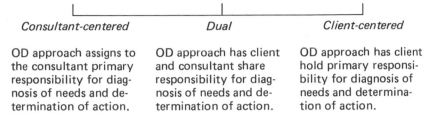

Consultant-centered	Dual	Client-centered
OD approach assigns to the consultant primary responsibility for diagnosis of needs and determination of action.	OD approach has client and consultant share responsibility for diagnosis of needs and determination of action.	OD approach has client hold primary responsibility for diagnosis of needs and determination of action.

zational activity is its contribution to profit. Such activities as production and sales can be measured in terms of their direct contribution to bottom-line profits. Line functions can usually be measured in this fashion. For staff functions such as personnel management or data processing, measurement of their contribution to profit is, at best, ill-defined and indirect. For these, process performance is a more appropriate measure than product performance. This divergence suggests the importance of multiple performance criteria.

Product-oriented performance criteria measure performance in terms of contribution to production and profit. *Process-oriented* performance criteria measure performance in nonproduction, nonsales terms and usually deal with the quality of organizational processes. Some organizational activities contribute both directly and indirectly to profit and should be measured by *product-process* criteria.

Each approach to OD carries with it different criteria for the measurement of its success. For example, sensitivity training would not improve production but should contribute to profit by improving processes. Thus, when sensitivity training is used as an approach to OD, its success should be measured by process-oriented performance criteria. The full range of performance criteria by which managers differentiate between alternative approaches to OD is illustrated in Figure 9.

Figure 9. The nature of performance criteria in OD approaches.

Product-oriented	Product- / Process-oriented	Process-oriented
OD approach measured by direct contributions to profit.	OD approach measured by direct and indirect contributions to profit.	OD approach measured by indirect contributions to profit.

The seven preceding managerial measures of OD constitute an OD scorecard. With this scorecard (Figure 10) managers can rate approaches to OD in the dimensions important to them and their organization. They are: plan,

Figure 10. Managerial measures of OD approaches.

Alternative Approaches to OD	Nature of the Plan (Fig. 2) Structured Sequentially structured Unstructured	Nature of Power (Fig. 4) Unilateral Shared Delegated	Nature of Personal Relationships (Fig. 5) Impersonal Personal-Work Personal	Nature of Pace (Fig. 6) Evolutionary Incremental Rapid	Nature of Price (Fig. 7) Inexpensive Moderate Expensive	Nature of Professional Relationships (Fig. 8) Client centered Dual Consultant centered	Nature of Performance Criteria (Fig. 9) Product Product-Process Process

power, personal relationships, pace, price, professional relationships, and performance criteria.

A completed scorecard allows managers to scan the profiles of alternative approaches to OD and select the most appropriate one. To do this managers must have an accurate description of each alternative approach to OD. In Chapter 5, six currently popular approaches to OD are defined, illustrated with cases, and rated on the scorecard. The completed ratings provide an OD "consumer's guide" for operating managers to help them decide what to buy. But before making that decision, the manager must know whether he needs to buy anything. He must first collect data about his organization and its problems. Here, too, he has options, which are described in detail in the next chapter.

CHAPTER 4

Diagnosing for OD

OD was earlier explained as a process of asking and answering three questions: Where are we? Where do we want to be? How do we get from where we are to where we want to be? These questions constitute phases of OD. The diagnostic phase asks and answers "Where are we?" and "Where do we want to be?" The intervention phase asks and answers "How do we get from where we are to where we want to be?" Some consultants also speak of an eventual maintenance phase in which the organization continues such questioning on a regular basis. This third phase is not common to all OD approaches and will be mentioned here only when it appears as part of a specific approach.

The diagnostic phase of any OD effort answers its questions through data collection and analysis. The intervention phase takes corrective action based on the data collected. Approaches to OD are differentiated by the interventions employed—that is, by what is done to bring about movement from "where we are" to "where we want to be." The differentiation is by the type of intervention, rather than by diagnostic method, for several reasons. To begin with, interventions vary widely from one OD approach to another, while diagnostic methods are more universal. Also, there are fewer diagnostic techniques to choose from than there are interventions, which makes the intervention a more precise differentiation. Moreover, an OD approach may use any of the available diagnostic methods, but it will usually employ only one kind of intervention. Therefore, it is best to treat diagnosis first, as a general category of activity relevant to all OD, then go on to consider interventions in much more specific terms.

This chapter, then, identifies criteria which can help managers choose the diagnostic method most appropriate to their needs, and explains alternative data collection techniques. The initial pages introduce four dimensions of data collection that can be used as managerial yardsticks. The remaining and major part of the chapter discusses the three most common data collection techniques: questionnaires, interviews, and observations. Each technique is illustrated and examined for its strengths and weaknesses.

MANAGERIAL DIMENSIONS OF DATA COLLECTION

There are basically three ways to gather data. You can ask written questions (the questionnaire). You can ask oral questions (the interview). You can watch what people do (direct observation). Each method varies in form from simple to highly sophisticated. Even complex variations—such as "organizational mirroring" or "group sensing"—remain variants of these three basic methods.

Because OD approaches are relatively flexible in means of data collection, a manager can choose the diagnostic method best suited to his organization. To do this, he needs to know the properties of the various techniques and their effects on his organization. It is not necessary for him to know the details of sampling techniques, the science of questionnaire development, or the many potential frameworks for data analysis—these are the skills of the data technician. But it is of utmost importance for him to consider the conditions under which organization members will reveal problems of personal and organizational significance. He must know how his people will be approached in order to conjecture how they will respond. He must, with the consultant, seek a collection method that will elicit meaningful data.

Here are some questions managers can use as criteria to assess different data collection techniques.

"Is it direct or indirect?" This determines how close to its source the data is collected. Direct methods are firsthand and accurate, but require high trust. Indirect methods are secondhand, often anonymous, but offer maximum privacy for the respondent and require no trust.

"Is it structured or unstructured?" This evaluates the freedom of expression available to respondents. Structured methods force respondents to choose among given, and therefore preselected, alternatives. Unstructured methods allow respondents to answer as they see fit.

"Is it more or less time consuming?" This establishes the amount of time required to prepare, gather, and analyze the data.

"Is it easy or difficult to administer?" This defines the level of skill required to prepare, gather, and analyze the data.

The manager should consider alternative data collection methods in light of these questions and of their impact on the willingness and ability of his people to respond. To clarify the choice available to managers, the three basic diagnostic methods are described below in these contexts.

The Survey Questionnaire

This is the diagnostic tool most frequently used in OD. Questionnaires are universally employed, for so many purposes, that their uses, costs, and benefits are familiar to most managers.

Questionnaires are generally indirect means of collecting specific kinds of information. Most often they are completed anonymously. One advantage of anonymity is that protection of respondents' identities often brings out strong feelings or opinions that would not be expressed openly, but which have significant effects on individuals' behavior in the organization. However, anonymity, by concealing exactly who feels or thinks what, may obscure the locus of problems or discontent. Indirectness also means that it is difficult to pursue issues in depth through follow-up discussion, thus the resultant data may be very superficial.

Questionnaires are structured data collection devices that usually require a forced-choice response. For example,

Do you feel your superior is:

        Too strict____Strict____ Fair____Easy____Too easy____?

Such structuring allows easy administration, makes minimal demands on respondents' time, and facilitates quantification of results for statistical analysis. At the same time, forced-choice structuring can be uninformative, rigid, and impersonal. Highly structured questionnaires are a poor substitute for real communication in identifying individuals' problems and concerns. This can be partially alleviated by making questionnaires open-ended, thus allowing respondents more freedom to express their individual feelings and opinions. Where this is done, data collection is more time consuming and analysis is much more difficult—imagine recording and coordinating the variety of responses to the open-ended question, "How does your supervisor treat you?"

In a managers' choice of a diagnostic tool, considerations of form, important as they are, do not match the importance of content. A questionnaire is only as valuable as the questions it asks are appropriate to the organization and its members. Too often this important common-sense point is overlooked in the rush to gather diagnostic data quickly and economically. For this reason, managers should be acquainted with the variety of survey content available. The critical considerations here are standardization versus originality, and climate versus issue.

Rensis Likert's "Profile of Organizational Characteristics" is perhaps the best known and most widely used of the standardized organizational climate questionnaires.[1] Questionnaires of this type are developed to measure the

[1]*New Patterns of Management* (New York: McGraw-Hill, 1961), pp. 223–233.

total organizational atmosphere or climate of any organization. They are usually organized around certain key variables. In Likert's profile these are character of motivational forces, communication processes, interactional processes,
decision-making processes, goal-setting processes, control processes, and performance characteristics. Other questionnaires may, of course, use other variables, but they all have in common a concern for the total organizational climate.

The full Likert profile is much too lengthy for inclusion here. A shorter,
much less time-consuming form, the "Management diagnosis chart," is illustrated in Figure 11. It was adapted by Likert himself.

A general measurement of organizational climate is most appropriate when
there is a feeling that something is wrong but no insight has developed into
just what the problem is. Climate questionnaires such as Likert's are also helpful in determining preferred general directions of organizational change. The
advantages of a standardized climate questionnaire are its ready availability
(hence its minimum development cost) and the ease of comparing results with
those of other organizations and other climates. However, the format or content of a standardized instrument may not be appropriate for assessing the
climate of a particular organization. Where this is the case, an original organizational climate questionnaire may be in order.

The original organizational climate questionnaire illustrated in Figure 12
was developed by a consultant and the managers of one company (here disguised as the DPD Company) to meet its particular diagnostic needs. The
managers were especially concerned about certain areas they felt were unique
to the DPD climate. These included interdepartmental cooperation and the
"fit" between the individual and the organization. Such issues were not adequately addressed in the standardized questionnaires they reviewed, so they
decided to develop their own diagnostic survey. With the consultant they
identified areas of key organizational climate variables, and within each area
the range of alternative behavior patterns was defined. Employees were asked
to indicate what behavior best described DPD at present and what behavior
would be ideal. The return on the DPD managers' considerable investment of
time and energy was an organizational climate questionnaire specifically suited
to their company and the unique variables affecting its climate.

The relative costs and benefits of standardized versus original questionnaires
are important considerations for managers in selecting data collection methods.
Another important point of choice is the possibility of using issue-oriented
questionnaires as an alternative to a general evaluation of organizational climate. In many cases evaluation of the general atmosphere of the organization
is unnecessary. The problems may be so readily apparent that what is needed
is more specific, in-depth data collection. Questionnaires oriented toward

Figure 11.   Management diagnosis chart.

		Present State		Desired State	
LEADERSHIP	How much confidence is shown in subordinates?	None	Condescending	Substantial	Complete
	How free do they feel to talk to superiors about job?	Not at all	Not very	Rather free	Fully free
	Are subordinates' ideas sought and used, if worthy?	Seldom	Sometimes	Usually	Always
MOTIVATION	Is predominant use made of (1) fear, (2) threats, (3) punishment, (4) rewards, (5) involvement?	1, 2, 3, occasionally 4	4, some 3	4, some 3 and 5	5, 4, based on group-set goals
	Where is responsibility felt for achieving organization's goals?	Mostly at top	Top and middle	Fairly general	At all levels
COMMUNICATION	How much communication is aimed at achieving organization's objectives?	Very little	Little	Quite a bit	A great deal
	What is the direction of information flow?	Downward	Mostly downward	Down and up	Down, up, and sideways
	How is downward communication accepted?	With suspicion	Possibly with suspicion	With caution	With an open mind
	How accurate is upward communication?	Often wrong	Censored for the boss	Limited accuracy	Accurate
	How well do superiors know problems faced by subordinates?	Know little	Some knowledge	Quite well	Very well
DECISIONS	At what level are decisions formally made?	Mostly at top	Policy at top, some delegation	Broad policy at top, more delegation	Throughout but well integrated
	What is the origin of technical and professional knowledge used in decision making?	Top management	Upper and middle	To a certain extent, throughout	To a great extent, throughout
	Are subordinates involved in decisions related to their work?	Not at all	Occasionally consulted	Generally consulted	Fully involved
	What does decision-making process contribute to motivation?	Nothing, often weakens it	Relatively little	Some contribution	Substantial contribution
GOALS	How are organizational goals established?	Orders issued	Orders, some comment invited	After discussion, by orders	By group action (except in crisis)
	How much covert resistance to goals is present?	Strong resistance	Moderate resistance	Some resistance at times	Little or none
CONTROL	How concentrated are review and control functions?	Highly at top	Relatively highly at top	Moderate delegation to lower levels	Quite widely shared
	Is there an informal organization resisting the formal one?	Yes	Usually	Sometimes	No—same goals as formal
	What are cost, productivity, and other control data used for?	Policing, punishment	Reward and punishment	Reward, some self-guidance	Self-guidance, problem solving

Figure 12. DPD organizational values and behavior.

The DPD Company is an organization of interdependent, interrelated units. Managing here is a continuing process and results are caused by this process and by the effectiveness of the total system. Although individuals, including administrators, within the system are quite different, individual behavior is largely determined by organizational forces, norms, and values, and by the managing process used. This form is designed to identify some of the organization's values and behavior patterns which significantly affect the ability of the organization to reach its business objectives.

Please place an X along each of the scales below at the position which you think best indicates the present DPD pattern or norm. This can be at A or B or anywhere in between. Then place a check mark ($\sqrt{}$) at the position you feel would be ideal for our organization.

1. Think about the kind of authority used. Some may rely on the authority of their positions to make decisions, to act, and to control, or on the power of their titles to influence decisions or actions. Others rely on knowledge, competence, and rightness for the situation. The authority most often used here at present (X) and the authority which would be ideal ($\sqrt{}$) are:

Authority of position; dependence on the boss.   A |⎵⎸⎵⎸⎵⎸⎵⎸⎵| B   Authority of competence; authority of knowledge.

2. Group and functional relationships and communications.

   a. Intergroup isolation, competition, boundary confusion. Little is done about problems between departments; they continue to exist.   A |⎵⎸⎵⎸⎵⎸⎵⎸⎵| B   Overlap between groups is used as opportunity for creativity, cooperation, and "interface" management. Problems between departments are worked through toward cooperative effort and understanding.

   b. Maskmanship and game playing (strategy and outmaneuvering); diplomacy, not saying what one thinks or expressing what one feels; avoiding facing others with data relevant to them.   A |⎵⎸⎵⎸⎵⎸⎵⎸⎵| B   Open, real relationships; authentic expression of feelings; leveling; directness; congruence; high trust.

   c. Managerial communications follow rigid organization lines. Orders come down, but there is little upward flow. People are unaware of the organization's or others' objectives, goals, and activities. Information is ferreted out. Rumors and information abound.   A |⎵⎸⎵⎸⎵⎸⎵⎸⎵| B   Communications are open and direct. Information about objectives, goals, and activities is shared. To get the job done, people feel free to contact others at higher and lower levels and in other functions.

3. Handling of conflicts and differences.

Denial of smoothing over, or suppression of conflict, or indirect conflict.   A |⎵⎸⎵⎸⎵⎸⎵⎸⎵| B   Direct confrontation of differences.

4. Use of rewards and controls:

Overdependence on external rewards and controls; close supervision; pressure from the boss.   A |⎵⎸⎵⎸⎵⎸⎵⎸⎵| B   Self-direction and -control; pressure from the situation.

5. Attitude toward organizational goals:

Low level of aspiration; indifference about goals.   A |⎵⎸⎵⎸⎵⎸⎵⎸⎵| B   High level of aspiration; enthusiasm about goals.

Figure 12 (continued)

6. Planning and action for personal growth.

Dependence for career planning and growth—people think that if they "keep their noses clean" the company will take care of them. A|_|_|_|_|_|_|_| B Initiative and exercise of individual choice about career and growth.

7. Status and symbols of status:

Status and symbols of status are used for narrowly personal ends, to hide behind, and to maintain the aura of power and prestige. Name dropping (use of authority figure) is one of the weapons for getting something accomplished. A|_|_|_|_|_|_|_| B Status is used for organizationally relevant purposes. People do not work out a problem by invoking the name of a senior executive—it's not *who* but *what* is right. Status symbols recognize knowledge, responsibility, and function, and are not used to build walls and block communications.

8. Willingness to accept responsibility and take risks, to experiment:

People avoid putting themselves or their groups on the line. There is great reliance on conformity, tradition, and past practice. There is excessive caution and defensiveness. A|_|_|_|_|_|_|_| B People feel that they have the right to fail. They are willing to put themselves on line to try something new and different, to take chances, and to face the consequences of their choices.

9. Evaluation of performance:

Performance is evaluated wholly on the basis of such inputs as how busy a man is, how fast he moves, whether he is always on time, whether he works long hours. A|_|_|_|_|_|_|_| B Performance is evaluated wholly on the basis of such outputs as what a man accomplishes, whether he creates improvements, how productive his team is, how fast his people develop, whether he achieves his objectives.

10. Top management style:

The top executives of DPD tend to behave mostly in reaction to problems and pressures. Things change only when top management finally recognizes something has to be done. A|_|_|_|_|_|_|_| B Top DPD management anticipates problems in advance, is active in initiating change before someone else insists, and is actively attempting to influence the environment that influences DPD.

11. How mistakes are used:

When DPD personnel make errors or mistakes, their supervisors tend to punish. In the system it is important to avoid being punished. A|_|_|_|_|_|_|_| B Supervisors tend to use errors or mistakes as opportunities to coach and train their subordinates.

specific issues are also frequently employed to examine areas of concern revealed in a general climate survey. Here again the manager may choose between standardized and original surveys.

Figure 13 is a standardized organizational issue questionnaire on job satisfaction. Like the Likert general profile, the issues-oriented questionnaire is designed around key variables, which are, in this case, fulfillment, salary, and recognition. The results are easily quantified and can be compared between jobs, departments, companies, or industries.

Figure 14 is an original job satisfaction questionnaire designed for a department of a municipal government. Of particular interest is this questionnaire's attempt to probe employees' feelings and opinions about city employment as well as about their specific jobs and department. At issue for this organization was the question, "Is job satisfaction or dissatisfaction related to the city, to the department, or to both?" On finding that no standardized job satisfaction questionnaire adequately addressed this question, they created one of their own.

Figures 11 through 14 represent, of course, only four of literally hundreds of available questionnaires. However, they do illustrate the four basic varieties of questionnaires—standardized climate, original climate, standardized issue, and original issue. These varieties identify *what* can be asked. Earlier discussion described *how* questions are asked. Both the what and the how of questionnaires—their content and their form—affect the kind and quality of responses gathered. The manager must consider both as he looks for a data collection method under which his people will most effectively reveal the significant problems of the organization. The major pros and cons of the content and form of questionnaires are reviewed in Figure 15.

Interviews

Interviews are direct means of collecting information through purposeful conversation between an interviewer and one or more respondents. If there is more than one respondent, it is a group interview, sometimes referred to in OD work as "organizational sensing." In a typical interview, questions structured to elicit responses about areas of concern are presented in face-to-face conversation either with key organizational members or with a representative sample of members.

The directness of the interview technique is both its strongest asset and its greatest liability. The immediacy of face-to-face interaction makes it possible for items of interest to be explored in depth immediately and in the context in which they arise. This enhances the accuracy of diagnosis and ensures that members' actual feelings and attitudes are being gathered. Respondents may

Figure 13. Standard job satisfaction questionnaire.

This questionnaire asks you to give three ratings to nine aspects of your job. Each rating is to be made on a seven-point scale ranging from minimum to maximum. Circle the number on the scale that represents the amount of each characteristic you think you have or want. If you think there is very little or none of the characteristic now associated with your job, you would circle 1. If you think there is just a little, you would circle 2, and so on. If you think there is a great deal but not a maximum amount, you would circle 6. On each scale, circle only one number.

	Mini-mum						Maxi-mum
1. Interesting work.							
(a) How much is there now?	1	2	3	4	5	6	7
(b) How much should there be?	1	2	3	4	5	6	7
(c) How important is this to you?	1	2	3	4	5	6	7
2. Opportunity to use one's skill.							
(a) How much is there now?	1	2	3	4	5	6	7
(b) How much should there be?	1	2	3	4	5	6	7
(c) How important is this to you?	1	2	3	4	5	6	7
3. Opportunity to experience a sense of accomplishment.							
(a) How much is there now?	1	2	3	4	5	6	7
(b) How much should there be?	1	2	3	4	5	6	7
(c) How important is this to you?	1	2	3	4	5	6	7
4. Salary.							
(a) How much is there now?	1	2	3	4	5	6	7
(b) How much should there be?	1	2	3	4	5	6	7
(c) How important is this to you?	1	2	3	4	5	6	7
5. Opportunity to serve others.							
(a) How much is there now?	1	2	3	4	5	6	7
(b) How much should there be?	1	2	3	4	5	6	7
(c) How important is this to you?	1	2	3	4	5	6	7
6. Recognition in current job.							
(a) How much is there now?	1	2	3	4	5	6	7
(b) How much should there be?	1	2	3	4	5	6	7
(c) How important is this to you?	1	2	3	4	5	6	7
7. Promotions.							
(a) How much is there now?	1	2	3	4	5	6	7
(b) How much should there be?	1	2	3	4	5	6	7
(c) How important is this to you?	1	2	3	4	5	6	7
8. Pleasant co-workers.							
(a) How much is there now?	1	2	3	4	5	6	7
(b) How much should there be?	1	2	3	4	5	6	7
(c) How important is this to you?	1	2	3	4	5	6	7
9. Job stability.							
(a) How much is there now?	1	2	3	4	5	6	7
(b) How much should there be?	1	2	3	4	5	6	7
(c) How important is this to you?	1	2	3	4	5	6	7

Your age_____   Time in company _____

Your education_____ Time in present job _____

Figure 14. People effectiveness survey.

This survey will be used to help us understand how City employees feel about our effectiveness in working with people. Please complete this questionnaire (anonymously).

How to answer: After reading each statement, mark an X in one of the four boxes that best describes how you feel about that statement. Circle the ? only if you have no opinion, or if the statement does not apply to you, or if the statement is not clear.

	Strongly Disagree	Disagree	Agree	Strongly Agree	
1. My work is satisfying to me.	☐	☐	☐	☐	?
2. There is not enough cooperation between my work group and others we work with.	☐	☐	☐	☐	?
3. There are opportunities in the City for those who want to get ahead.	☐	☐	☐	☐	?
4. For the jobs in my areas, working conditions are O.K.	☐	☐	☐	☐	?
5. We don't get enough information about how well our work group is doing.	☐	☐	☐	☐	?
6. Many City employees I know would like to see the union get in.	☐	☐	☐	☐	?
7. The City's retirement plan is O.K.	☐	☐	☐	☐	?
8. I can be sure of a job with the City as long as I do good work.	☐	☐	☐	☐	?
9. There are too many City rules and procedures to follow.	☐	☐	☐	☐	?
10. I have as much freedom as I need to do my job well.	☐	☐	☐	☐	?
11. I feel free to tell my supervisor what I think.	☐	☐	☐	☐	?
12. I am proud to work for the City.	☐	☐	☐	☐	?
13. I am paid fairly for the kind of work I do.	☐	☐	☐	☐	?
14. During the past six months I have looked for a job outside the City.	☐	☐	☐	☐	?
15. Favoritism is a problem in my area.	☐	☐	☐	☐	?
16. Most City employees I know are in jobs that make good use of their abilities.	☐	☐	☐	☐	?
17. My job seems to be leading to the kind of future I want.	☐	☐	☐	☐	?
18. The City is a better place to work than it was last year.	☐	☐	☐	☐	?
19. I understand what is expected of me in my work.	☐	☐	☐	☐	?
20. Compared with private industries, the City's fringe benefits are good.	☐	☐	☐	☐	?
21. There are too many departmental rules and procedures to follow.	☐	☐	☐	☐	?

Figure 15. Pros and cons of questionnaires.

General properties	Positive attributes	Negative attributes
Indirect; anonymous, secondhand data gathering	Anonymity may encourage honesty and candor	May be difficult to determine precisely what feelings and opinions are held and/or where they are held
Structured; freedom of response usually restricted through forced choice	Data easily quantified, facilitating statistical analysis	Forced-choice response may miss real feelings and opinions
	Easy to handle many respondents	Difficult to pursue issues in depth
Not time consuming	Little time needed to administer, complete, and compile results	Rigid
	Inexpensive	
Easy to administer	Requires little skill to administer, inexpensive	

introduce provocative areas which the data collectors may not previously have thought to investigate, and these too can be pursued. The directness of interviews lends a degree of accuracy, depth, and flexibility not possible in survey questionnaires.

The major limitation of face-to-face interviews is that anonymous responses are not possible. Unless the respondent has complete trust in the interviewer, it is unlikely that the data revealed will be candid and honest. Two points must be kept firmly in mind—trust and rapport are essential to effective interviewing, but they are not easily established. These two points cannot be stressed too strongly in considering interviewing as a data collection device, for both deeply affect all other properties of interviewing as a diagnostic tool.

Like questionnaires, interviews vary in content and structure. The content alternatives of interviews are the same as those of questionnaires: standardized, original, climate, issue. Similarly, interviews may be structured, forced-choice, or open-ended. The usual pattern is the open-ended interview, allowing respondents to express whatever answer seems most appropriate to them, since this approach makes maximum use of the flexibility that is the major advantage of interviewing. Here are examples of the kinds of questions in open-ended interviews. When these general questions lead to points of particular interest, the interviewer may use more pointed questioning to guide the respondent into further elaboration.

1(a) What do you see as the ten most important problems in the organization?
 (b) How do these problems affect you and your work?
 (c) How would you solve them?
2(a) What do other people do that makes it difficult for you to work effectively?
 (b) What do you do that makes it difficult for others to work effectively?
3(a) If you were in charge, what would you *stop* doing today to make the organization more effective?
 (b) If you were in charge, what would you *start* doing today to make the organization more effective?

The questions asked in a structured interview are much more specific and detailed. There is usually a preset sequence of questions, with alternative follow-up questions for "yes" or "no" responses, and sometimes a prescribed length of time may be allowed for a response. Here are some sample questions from such a format. These examples are drawn from an interview that was designed to assess interest in participation in a "job enlargement" program.

1. As you probably know, there is going to be a job enlargement program. Are you signed up right now, so you can participate if you want to? (If the answer is "Yes," skip to Question 3; if it is "No" or "Don't know," ask:)
2. How much interest do you have in the program—would you say you are very interested, fairly interested, or not very interested? (If the answer is "Fairly" or "Not very" interested, go to Question 4; if "Very interested," ask:)
3. Why are you interested?
4. What have you heard about the program?
5. How certain are you right now that you will participate—very certain, fairly certain, may not, will not?

Structured interviews run many of the same risks as forced-choice questionnaires, for they can be rigid and inflexible and miss important informative opportunities. At the other extreme, open-ended interviews, while they are usually interesting and engaging, may range far afield and generate a lot of irrelevant data. Some work has been done with semistructured interviews, a format that tries to combine the advantages of structured and open-ended interviews.

In a semistructured interview for diagnosing an organization, the interviewer gives the respondent a deck of 64 three-by-five cards. On each of the cards there is a statement about the organization. The card also contains a number— 1, 2, 3, or 4—which corresponds to the general categories of organizational problems (particularly those relevant to teams) that are shown below. The respondent is asked to go through the deck and select the statements he feels are accurate for his organization. As he selects each one, he is asked to give a recent example illustrating it.

The respondent then puts the selected problems into three lists: (1) in order of importance, (2) in order of feasibility, or readiness, and (3) in order of personal influence on the respondent. These lists are coordinated and reported back to the respondents as a group.

Problem statements should be suited to the situation. The following list contains a broad sample, separated into four categories.

1. *Problems of organizational purpose and/or goals:*

There is observable resistance to the objectives of the organization.
There isn't the commitment to the organization that there used to be when we were smaller.
A number of organizational policies decrease the motivation of people.
The salary and wage area could certainly be improved.
We don't seem to be able to solve some of the organizational problems which have been with us for some time.
There is little communication of organizational objectives.
I don't know what is expected of me.
There is considerable pressure to conform to the official position on policy or issues.
Management really doesn't do very much to develop its people.
Policies and procedures are not clear.
Little direction is given.
We have little knowledge of the "big picture" in the organization.
We don't understand each other's goals and objectives.

2. *Problems of the distribution and structure of work:*

The work is too routine.
Meetings are too long and too poorly planned.
Job descriptions are poor.
I am uncertain of my authority.
There is little opportunity for advancement.
Information flow is mostly upward; not much information comes downward.
Subordinates' ideas at the lower levels of the organization are neither sought nor used very much.

There is little room to show initiative.

There is too much competitiveness between departments, which tends to build friction.

There is too much regulation.

I am unable to find and develop people of good potential in the organization.

Work is usually scheduled inefficiently.

There are too many different projects.

Information flow is mostly downward, not much information gets up to top management.

There's not enough to do.

We get no explanation of the "why" of work assignments.

Salary increases are more or less automatic, not related to performance.

Productivity, generally speaking, is well below its potential.

Management needs to be better organized.

Purchasing delays are a problem.

We don't feel that management trusts us.

3. *Problems of work processes:*

Leadership is too authoritarian.

We don't sufficiently utilize each other's abilities, knowledge, and experience.

There is a real complacency and apathy on the part of many workers.

There's no opportunity to speak to management except to the boss.

I have trouble getting subordinates to accept my authority and to follow orders when they are given.

Communication with my boss is poor.

We seem to be afraid to try out new ideas.

Newcomers are accepted reluctantly.

Top management is not very aware of problems faced at the working level.

We are not given credit for work accomplished.

There isn't much supervisory skill in management ranks.

Little communication takes place between departments.

We operate on the basis of "every man for himself."

Salaries are a very sensitive issue to talk about — we're too secretive.

The atmosphere is tense, probably due to the supervision we get.

Not much confidence is shown in lower-level supervision.

Our mode of operation is constant panic.

4. *Problems of personal and/or interpersonal processes:*

Sometimes we act as if we were highly suspicious of each other.

We are guarded and cautious in our organization and management discussions.

One of our biggest problems is simply people getting along with other people.

We tend to deny, avoid, or suppress conflicts.

There are certain important personality clashes in our organization.

I lack aggressiveness on my own part.

We don't really listen to each other.

The risk of being judged unfavorably gives me good reason to keep quiet and is a barrier in my work.

My reluctance to cause ill feelings or conflict prevents me from supervising as forcefully as sometimes I probably should.

Personal relations with supervisors are poor.

We don't respect each other's individual differences enough.

Personality conflicts between bosses and subordinates have too much weight in performance appraisals and merit.

There is too much favoritism unrelated to job performance.

Although they may vary in structure and content, interviews are universally time consuming. From the careful thought and consideration required for developing interview questions through setting the interview schedule, each step is time consuming and often frustrating. The interview itself requires considerable time for the interviewer and the interviewee alike, and shortening the time can adversely affect the development of trust between the interviewer and the respondent.

This all-important question of trust and rapport raises the final point to be made about interviewing as a data collection technique. They are *very* difficult to administer. Effective interviewing requires highly skilled interviewers who can establish the needed rapport quickly and who can direct the interview into areas of importance. It is rare to find these skills within organizations, and it is expensive to purchase them.

The pros and cons of interviews as a diagnostic data collection technique are summarized in Figure 16. Here, again, the manager must consider the effect of these conditions on his people and their willingness to reveal significant problems.

Direct Observation

This final general category includes diagnostic techniques that collect data about the organization by watching it at work. Time and motion studies are a familiar and often used form of direct observation data collection. Trained observers measure the time taken to perform specific motions, tasks, or activities. These times are recorded and analyzed to determine where and how improvements can be made. Time and motion studies are not, of course, the only forms of direct observation. Structured observational formats and organizational mirroring are two currently popular diagnostic methods.

Figure 16. Pros and cons of interviews.

General properties	Positive attributes	Negative attributes
Direct; firsthand, face-to-face data collection	Increased depth and flexibility	No anonymity
		Confrontive
	Interaction may facilitate implementation later	High trust required for candor
Relatively unstructured; seldom force choices, usually are open-ended	More freedom of response, thus more accurately showing feelings and opinions	Rambling
		May generate irrelevant data
		Difficult to quantify
Time consuming	Depth	Loss of time
	Involvement of respondent	
Difficult to administer; preparation, process, and analysis require highly skilled personnel	Trust, when developed, is a valuable asset	Necessary skills are scarce and expensive

Direct observation is, as the name suggests, a direct means of collecting data about what organization members actually do. It is a very indirect means of collecting data about what members actually think and/or feel about what they do, for inferences of feelings and opinions from observed behavior are obviously subject to serious error. However, observation is a very accurate means of recording what people actually do, because it is a firsthand, on-site, and real-time method.

The kinds of behavior recorded vary with the format of direct observation, as does the identification of the recorder. Figure 17 is an example of a structured format for observing group behavior. This very simple form is used to record who does what in group meetings, a record that often gives important insight into group work behavior from the perspective of group members. It describes how a group goes about its work.

Figure 18 is a more complicated form for recording the task and maintenance behavior of group members. This example is more typical of the kinds of direct observation diagnosis in OD work. The recorder is a trained observer, usually the consultant.

"Organizational mirroring" is a direct observation format used to record the observations, not of trained observers, but of individuals or organizations

Figure 17. Feedback checklist.

Comments on: _____ Date: _____

Behavior observed	Never				Always
	1	2	3	4	5
1. Contributes to discussion					
2. Displays alertness					
3. Shows interest in subject					
4. Effectively identifies problems					
5. Effectively solves identified problems					
6. Is effective in decision making					
7. Responds sensitively to others					
8. Exhibits good listening skills					
9. Is honest with self and others					
10. Expresses ideas clearly					
11. Exhibits objectivity					
12. Is supportive of others					
13. Recognizes important points					
14. Exhibits critical self-analysis					
15. Shows high commitment to learning					
16. Contributes to others' learning					
17. Keeps pace with discussion					
18. Stimulates thinking in others					
19. Is open-minded					
20. Is receptive to new ideas					
21. Is resourceful					
22. Is creative					
23. Is prompt with projects and assignments					
24. Uses time efficiently					
25. Has high standards of performance					

Figure 18. Feedback checklist on behavior.

Comments on:_____ Date:_____

Grade on a scale from 0 (never) to 9 (always)

Task Functions

Initiating	1. Is resourceful	_____
	2. Is creative	_____
Information seeking	3. Is receptive to new ideas	_____
	4. Stimulates thinking of others	_____
Information giving	5. Contributes to discussion	_____
	6. Shares relevant personal experiences	_____
	7. Makes pertinent comments	_____
Clarifying	8. Expresses ideas clearly	_____
	9. Recognizes important points	_____
Elaborating	10. Expands on topics	_____
Summarizing	11. Recognizes responsibility as learner and listener	_____
	12. Keeps pace with discussion	_____
Consensus testing	13. Questions group's decisions	_____

Maintenance functions:

Harmonizing	1. Is stable and at ease	_____
	2. Acts to relieve tension	_____
Compromising	3. Is open-minded	_____
	4. Is able to arbitrate	_____
Gatekeeping	5. Displays alertness	_____
	6. Utilizes time well	_____
Encouraging	7. Shows interest in subject	_____
	8. Hears others out willingly	_____
	9. Supports others' points	_____
Diagnosing	10. Exhibits critical self-analysis	_____
Standard setting	11. Has knowledge of assignments	_____
	12. Has high standards of performance	_____
Standard testing	13. Questions group norms	_____
	14. Questions group processes	_____

Leadership functions:

	1. Assumes leader's role	_____
	2. Exhibits personal confidence	_____
	3. Does not become defensive	_____
	4. Does not put others on the defensive	_____

who interface with the organization being examined. This enables organization members to learn how their performance and internal organizational processes are viewed by such observers as clients, other departments, or other organizations. In this era of consumerism, organizational mirroring has become an increasingly popular diagnostic tool. The following extended example gives the steps in diagnostic data collection through organizational mirroring.

1. Identify the relevant "publics" of the focal unit or organization.

2. Ask the different publics, via questionnaires or interviews, to describe the nature of their interaction with the focal organization.

3. Ask them to report *their observations* of key organizational processes. For example:

   (a) What is the business of_____and what should it be as it relates to your company or department?

   (b) What are some concerns you have in relating to_____?

   (c) What should_____
       Do more of:
       Do less of:
       Stop doing:
       Start doing:

4. Report responses back to the focal unit organization.

The responses reproduced below resulted from the use of organizational mirroring in an OD effort with the personnel department of a company with 6,000 employees. Members of other departments in the company were asked to respond to the questions in section 3 above. The responses are illustrative of the kinds of information revealed through organizational mirroring.

3(a) What is the purpose or business of the Personnel Department?
To set standard rules by which we work and penalties for deviation.
To act as a recruiting agency.
To provide technical and general training programs.
To be a connector between departments.
To be a source of information.
To take care of employee needs.
To provide service to departments in a timely manner.
To give final answers and be a clearinghouse for overall personnel matters.
To be a service department, rather than a dictator.

3(b) What are some concerns you have in relating to the Personnel
        Department?
      I do not like to feel it is another set of bosses.
      It should be part of our team to help us get the job done.
      We don't trust personnel, because we don't get the support we
        need.
      We aren't viewed as personnel.
      We are on the defensive when a proposal is made.
      We are made to feel we are not competent.
      Inferences are made that we are not managers of personnel.
      Personnel should be a supporting service to other departments.
      Too much time must be spent in justifying, battling, hassling, and
        debating.
      Our input should be more heavily weighted.
      It doesn't listen to our input.
      We are not benefiting from the training programs — especially super-
        visors.
      More training should be geared to lower levels.
      I get an answer from one person and then it is reversed by a
        manager.
      The interpretation you get depends on whom you call.
      The flow of paper is to the field or an individual or the office, and
        we may or may not get a copy.
      All personnel memos should be channeled through our adminis-
        trative office.
      We are unaware of the organization or divisions of personnel.
      We don't know very much about the Personnel Department.
      Often we are not in on the formation of administrative directives.
      We need more personal communication to interpret directives.

3(c) What should Personnel do more of? Do less of? Stop doing? Start
        doing?
      Streamline procedural processes; it takes forever to get something
        done.
      Give more consideration to the individual department's judgment.
      Stop frustrating our attempts to upgrade our department.
      Pay less attention to incumbents in positions and more to the
        positions.
      Respect our position and judgment — we are managers, but we are
        not listened to.
      Communicate more about what it is doing.
      Expand the training programs.
      Don't try to be the recreational or social leader for the city.
      Educate departments on how to make the system work.

Give more samples and aids for applying rules.

Give straightforward answers—it's hard to get a yes or a no.

Help us solve problems even when we are headed in the wrong direction.

Give more publicity to what can be done to help the employee.

Go to the field more, rather than have employees come downtown.

Establish better communications with departments.

Get out information quicker.

Have counselors contact supervisors more often about manpower enrollees.

Send all personnel matters to the department's central administrative unit.

Offer the guidance of professional personnel people.

Direct observation is a relatively structured means of data collection. Key categories of behavior are identified and trained observers classify activities into these categories. As in the case of questionnaires and interviews, the content of direct observation—that is, the categories chosen—may be common to all organizations or unique to one. To the extent that the chosen categories survey problem areas of behavior, this structure improves the accuracy of data collection. However, problems that fall outside these selected categories are often either ignored or noticed but not recorded.

Direct observation is a time-consuming means of collecting data, but it is not as time consuming as interviewing. The advantage of direct observation is that no work time is lost, for workers are observed in the actual performance of their jobs. But this observation can be a lengthy process.

For the most part, data collection by direct observation requires skilled trained observers, but this is less true where simple observation or organizational mirroring is used. Yet, even in the simplest cases, data analysis can be difficult.

In considering the use of direct observation to collect data about their organization, managers must keep in mind the basic properties identified above and their positive and negative effects. These are summarized in Figure 19.

At the outset, this chapter defined the diagnostic phase of OD as a process of asking and answering the questions "Where are we?" and "Where do we want to be?" How these questions are asked is a decision to be made by the manager and the consultant using as their primary criterion the question "Under what conditions will organization members reveal problems of personal and organizational significance?" The three data collection methods—questionnaires, interviews, and direct observation—create different conditions for the manager to consider.

Figure 19. Pros and cons of direct observation.

General properties	Positive attributes	Negative attributes
Direct; firsthand observation of behavior	Accurate measurement of on-site work behavior	Difficult to determine attitudes and feelings from observation of behavior
Indirect; feelings and attitudes inferred from observation of behavior		
Relatively structured; observation in predetermined behavior categories	Categories can highlight behavior problems	Behavior problems may fall outside of categories and be ignored
Time consuming; on-site, real-time observation	No time lost by employees	Observation may be a lengthy process
Difficult to administer; skill required to determine categories, make the observation, and analyze	Clear statement of behavior problems and their effects	Necessary skills are scarce and expensive

While these differences can help a manager choose the data collection method best suited to his people and his organization, alone they are insufficient guidelines. What is most important is the manager's knowledge of his people. What will make them most comfortable, a questionnaire? A face-to-face interview? Someone observing them? Whom do they trust? Do they want their feelings and opinions to be recorded openly or anonymously? What have they time for? How will they respond to skilled outsiders? What has been their past experience with questionnaires, interviews, or observations? The answers to these kinds of questions can help the manager choose the diagnostic method best suited to his organization, the one that best reveals where his organization is and where it wants to be.

The next OD phase takes up the question: "How do we get from where we are to where we want to be?" The answer changes the focus of OD from diagnosis to intervention, and the choice of alternative approaches available to managers expands and becomes more complex. Chapter 5 provides a manager's guide to OD interventions.

Alternative Approaches to OD: A Consumer's Guide for Managers

One of the great misunderstandings about OD is the notion that it is one single thing. A manager who reports a positive experience with OD is assumed to be referring to the same OD as the manager who reports a negative experience. More than once fellow managers have argued vigorously, hour after hour, over the effects of OD, only to discover that the activities they experienced as OD were quite different. The first point managers need to understand is that the many approaches to OD have characteristics and capabilities as varied as the clients employing them.

The many approaches to OD represent different answers to the basic intervention question: How do we get from where we are to where we want to be? As in the case of the diagnostic phase of OD, the manager and the consultant must choose the approach best suited to the needs of the organization. Knowledge of the available alternatives is a necessity if managers are to make effective choices. This chapter introduces managers to the seven most popular approaches to OD: (1) survey feedback, (2) process consultation, (3) team building, (4) laboratory training, (5) packaged programs, (6) socio-technical systems, and (7) transactional analysis. Each approach is defined, illustrated with a brief case, and scored on the managerial measures of OD approaches explained in Chapter 3. At the end of the chapter, all seven approaches are summarized together for comparison.

The purpose of this chapter is to give managers a "consumer's guide to OD." If they have a clear picture of how each OD approach would operate in their organizations, managers will be better prepared to select an approach.

THE SURVEY FEEDBACK APPROACH TO OD

The survey feedback (SF) technique is one of the oldest and most popular approaches to OD. It was originally developed by Floyd Mann at the Survey

Research Center, University of Michigan, in the 1950s.[1] While no specific data are available, it is probably safe to say that from 1960 to 1970 SF was used more often than all other approaches to OD combined, and its popularity continues today. Survey feedback may be used as a solitary strategy or, as it frequently is, in combination with one or more complementary approaches. Many consultants and managers see SF as the only approach; for them, survey feedback *is* OD.

Defining Survey Feedback

The popularity of this approach is largely due to its simplicity. Three steps define intervention through SF. First, information about the organization is gathered, usually via a *survey* of member attitudes and opinions. This is, of course, the diagnostic phase. In the second step, the survey results are reported to organizational units as *feedback*. Finally, the organizational units examine the survey data and consider future corrective actions to be taken, if any.

From these simple basic steps more sophisticated SF programs evolve. External consultants develop measuring devices to gather the most detailed data about the organization's functioning and its members' work lives. These data are then subjected to in-depth quantitative and qualitative analysis and reported back to the organization in a complex, interlocking chain of conferences.

Whether simple or sophisticated, SF OD universally proceeds in the same fashion. One manager described in a casual but effective way the essence of SF OD as it occurred in his organization: "The consultants came in, asked my people some questions, gave me the answers, said 'what do you want to do about it?' and left. But not before they'd left me with a whopping bill!" This casual definition vividly captures the essential flow of SF OD.

The manager who contemplates the SF approach to OD should look beyond both its popularity and its simplicity to its specific activities. It is these with which managers must live and work. Some of these activities are illustrated in the case study below.

A Survey Feedback OD Case

Action Service is the name given to the customer service division at the headquarters office of a national department store. The purpose of Action Service is to serve as a court of last resort for consumers' concerns and complaints. The service was instituted two years ago for the avowed purpose of improving customer service and customer relations. As an integral part of its

---

[1] Floyd C. Mann and Rensis Likert, "The Need for Research on the Communication of Research Results," *Human Organization,* Winter 1952, pp. 15–19.

public relations effort, the company has promoted Action Service heavily in its advertising.

The operations of Action Service are simple, direct, and standardized. They are initiated by receipt of a consumer's complaint either through the mail or by telephone. Action Service is often the first place a consumer brings his complaint, but just as often it is the last in a long line of offices to which the consumer has complained. In either case, Action Service records the nature and details of the consumer's complaint and routes four copies to (1) Action Service files, (2) the complainant, (3) the vice-president of branch operations, and (4) the manager of the store where the complaint originated. Upon receipt of Action Service notices (known by store managers as "greenies" for the paper color of the form), managers are *required* to report to the VP of branch operations within ten days what corrective action they have taken.

A staff of 30 is assigned to Action Service. Their efforts are overseen by a manager and two assistant managers, the former reporting directly to the VP of branch operations. Staff turnover has averaged 10 percent a month, and at the time of this OD case only 10 staff members, one an assistant manager, had been with Action Service since it began. The manager had been appointed three months earlier after the original manager left the company. The new manager was not only new to Action Service, but new to the company, as well.

The appointment of the new manager came at a turning point for Action Service, a time when "greenies" were fewer and more customer complaints were being handled at the point of complaint. For this reason the purpose of Action Service was being reevaluated. Pat Gilbert, VP of branch operations, had handpicked the new manager of Action Service, Sam Hunter, more for his public relations background than for his administrative skills. Gilbert's intention was that under Hunter Action Service should begin to play a stronger PR role and shape consumer attitudes toward the store instead of merely respond to consumer complaints.

At this point things began to go wrong. In the three months immediately preceding and the three months following Hunter's takeover, turnover averaged 30 percent per month. Absenteeism and tardiness became significant problems. Three out of ten greenies filed by Action Service were not received by store managers. Gilbert and Hunter both began to ask, What's wrong? Was the problem Hunter? The employees? The nature of the work? Something had to be done immediately or the good work Action Service had performed would all be lost, but what should be done? They decided to contact a consultant to find a way to improve Action Service.

Gilbert, Hunter, and the consultant decided to use the short form of Likert's organization profile as an initial data collection strategy. They felt such a general survey would be the fastest and least expensive approach. The Likert form was also viewed as nonthreatening and as promising to yield the broadest possible picture of organizational problems. All 30 employees were given questionnaires to be completed at their leisure and returned anonymously to the consultant's office. A summary of employees' responses is presented in Figure 20.

The employees reported problems in virtually every area measured by the profile: leadership, motivation, communication, decisions, goals, and control. In each instance employees reported current Action Service practices far short of what they would like to see. The summary data were first presented to Gilbert and Hunter. They admitted to being overwhelmed by the number of problems identified. As Gilbert said, "It looks like there's so much wrong. What's more important? Where should we start? Should we start at all or scrap the whole thing? What's next?"

The consultant suggested that they look for guidance from the people who would ultimately be expected to implement improvement, the employees themselves. The suggested plan was to present the data to the employees and invite them to define priorities and to decide what, if anything, should be done. This classic SF design was approved by Gilbert and Hunter. They particularly liked the idea of presenting the data to Action Service groups composed of an assistant manager and his subordinates. There would be three groups, and all employees would ultimately be involved.

The consultant facilitated the feedback in a pattern identical for each employee group. A summary of the data was presented to the group and participants were invited to discuss the data, to make their interpretations, and to state what they felt ought to be done. Each group reported relief and appreciation that employees' concerns were finally out in the open. Each group also decided to rank the problems in the order of their importance to the group. The discussion over priorities was so long and heated that the groups agreed to withhold further discussion and action until their lists had been compared. Here are the three lists:

Group A	*Group B*	*Group C*
1. Goals	1. Goals	1. Goals
2. Decisions	2. Leadership	2. Communication
3. Communication	3. Motivation	3. Leadership
4. Leadership	4. Control	4. Motivation
5. Control	5. Communication	5. Decisions
6. Motivation	6. Decisions	6. Control

Figure 20. Action Service management diagnosis chart.

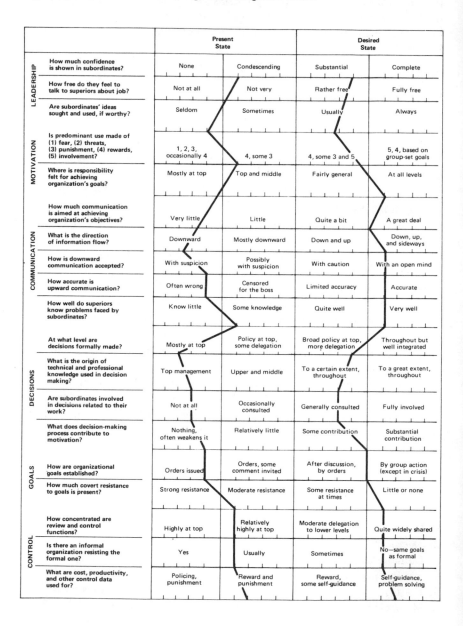

		Present State		Desired State	
LEADERSHIP	How much confidence is shown in subordinates?	None	Condescending	Substantial	Complete
	How free do they feel to talk to superiors about job?	Not at all	Not very	Rather free	Fully free
	Are subordinates' ideas sought and used, if worthy?	Seldom	Sometimes	Usually	Always
MOTIVATION	Is predominant use made of (1) fear, (2) threats, (3) punishment, (4) rewards, (5) involvement?	1, 2, 3, occasionally 4	4, some 3	4, some 3 and 5	5, 4, based on group-set goals
	Where is responsibility felt for achieving organization's goals?	Mostly at top	Top and middle	Fairly general	At all levels
COMMUNICATION	How much communication is aimed at achieving organization's objectives?	Very little	Little	Quite a bit	A great deal
	What is the direction of information flow?	Downward	Mostly downward	Down and up	Down, up, and sideways
	How is downward communication accepted?	With suspicion	Possibly with suspicion	With caution	With an open mind
	How accurate is upward communication?	Often wrong	Censored for the boss	Limited accuracy	Accurate
	How well do superiors know problems faced by subordinates?	Know little	Some knowledge	Quite well	Very well
DECISIONS	At what level are decisions formally made?	Mostly at top	Policy at top, some delegation	Broad policy at top, more delegation	Throughout but well integrated
	What is the origin of technical and professional knowledge used in decision making?	Top management	Upper and middle	To a certain extent, throughout	To a great extent, throughout
	Are subordinates involved in decisions related to their work?	Not at all	Occasionally consulted	Generally consulted	Fully involved
	What does decision-making process contribute to motivation?	Nothing, often weakens it	Relatively little	Some contribution	Substantial contribution
GOALS	How are organizational goals established?	Orders issued	Orders, some comment invited	After discussion, by orders	By group action (except in crisis)
	How much covert resistance to goals is present?	Strong resistance	Moderate resistance	Some resistance at times	Little or none
CONTROL	How concentrated are review and control functions?	Highly at top	Relatively highly at top	Moderate delegation to lower levels	Quite widely shared
	Is there an informal organization resisting the formal one?	Yes	Usually	Sometimes	No—same goals as formal
	What are cost, productivity, and other control data used for?	Policing, punishment	Reward and punishment	Reward, some self-guidance	Self-guidance, problem solving

Feedback of these lists led to further group discussions. The importance of goal-related problems was evident to everyone involved, but within the groups there was considerable debate over whether they had sufficient data to begin to talk about solutions. In these discussions the consultant clarified and pointed out gaps in the available data. In survey feedback OD the consultant does not act alone or push for action, but instead tries to facilitate the groups' discussion of their own data and intentions.

In their second round of discussions, the Action Service groups made two decisions. The first was that further discussions and action should be through collective representatives rather than in separate groups. The second was that more data on goal-related problems were needed before action steps could be designed. Representatives from each group were selected, with Gilbert and Hunter included. This group was charged with collecting and reporting data on three key questions: How are goals for Action Service determined? What are the goals, as management sees them and as employees see them? What do employees think the goals should be?

This SF OD effort continued beyond what is recorded here. Ultimately Action Service adopted a dual structure to achieve its dual functions, customer service and public relations. The specific outcome of this brief case is less important here than the process it illustrates, a classic example of the survey feedback approach.

Scoring Survey Feedback OD

In the Action Service case, as in all survey feedback OD work, the process which occurred was an interlocking chain of conferences about data collected from the organization. The feedback intervention began with the reporting of findings to top management and descended through the organization to supervisors and employees, who discussed the data. These feedback meetings were structured by functional work groups according to organizational units. At each point, group members were asked to interpret the results—that is, to say what the data meant to them—to determine whether anything more should be done in response to the data. In Action Service it was decided to act on the data, but many times groups decide to do nothing; in either case, the survey feedback approach is completed.

This summary of the Action Service case describes a typical SF effort. The approach may vary with individual consultants and organizations, but the key features remain the same. The central property of the survey feedback approach, the use of data presentations as interventions, as vehicles for bringing about change, is the key point in managers' understanding of the survey feedback approach. The survey is the OD diagnostic phase, and the feedback of results is the intervention phase. The greater awareness of organization problems brought about by the feedback often leads directly to action planning. Just as often the organization chooses not to act on the data. Action is completely the prerogative of the organization; it is not a necessary or inevitable result of the survey feedback approach.

In addition to understanding the basic thrust of SF, managers need to know how this approach measures up against the critical choice criteria explained in Chapter 3: plan, power, personal relationships, pace, price, professional relationships, and performance criteria.

The survey feedback approach is rather rigidly planned and programmed, with little deviation from the detailed progression through data collection to phased data feedback meetings from the top down. This clearly defined procedure is one of the great attractions of SF to many managers, who find security in its standard, highly *structured* approach.

In the SF approach power is *unilateral,* to be shared only at the discretion of those in top management. In SF power takes the form of the information collected, which is first reported to those at the top, then filtered down through the organization only as they see fit. Survey feedback is decidedly a top-down approach to organizational change.

Survey feedback also tends to be an *impersonal* approach to OD. Typical data collection methods in SF seldom inquire into the personal relationships of employees. Often the importance of personal relationships in the work situation emerges as data are fed back to work groups. This is not designed into this approach, however. Concentration on impersonal data is far more characteristic of survey feedback.

As feedback moves through the organization from the top downward, new data are generated and new actions taken. The process gains momentum if it does not meet with resistance. This *incremental* pace of SF OD is another of its attractions for practicing managers. There is great pragmatic appeal in avoiding trying to do too much, too fast.

Depending upon the specific data collection methods used, SF is a *moderately* priced approach to OD. The actual data collection process can be lengthy, and feedback meetings are by necessity time consuming, but in tightly scheduled SF programs the time required for these steps is seldom excessive. Obviously, as employee participation increases, costs increase as well.

Data collection in survey feedback is very much a *consultant*-centered activity. The consultant guides the questioning to determine what is wrong. Once the data are collected and returned to the organization, the consultant removes himself from the picture, allowing the *client* system to determine what action, if any, should be taken. Yet another feature of SF attractive to managers is the control it gives them over the process of change.

Finally, the effectiveness of the SF approach to OD is measured by *process* criteria. SF is considered successful if data collected about the organization are effectively communicated to the members. The emphasis is on the feedback process, not on action that the feedback may evoke; thus SF OD does not insure that any action will be taken. This passive character is often considered by managers to be the major drawback of SF OD.

THE PROCESS CONSULTATION APPROACH TO OD

The process consultation (PC) approach to OD, developed by Edgar Schein, is practiced widely by a large number of consultants in organizations of every description. It is one of the primary approaches to increasing the effectiveness of managerial work groups. For this reason it may have particular interest for the operating manager who has problems at the top.

Defining Process Consultation

Schein defines PC as "a set of activities on the part of the consultant which help the client to perceive, understand, and act upon process events which occur in the clients' environment."[2]

The process consultation OD approach assumes that effective organizational performance depends upon effective human processes, and that when organization performance falters it is because critical human processes have broken down at key points in the organization. Some of these critical human processes are listed below along with questions to be asked when examining them:

Communication. How does information flow among members of the organization? (That is, *how* is content communicated, not *what* content is communicated?)

Member roles and functions in groups. Who does what, and how is it done, as the group goes about its work?

Group problem solving and decision making. How does the managerial group approach the resolution of problems? How does it arrive at decisions?

Group norms. What formal and informal rules guide behavior in the group? How do they affect what the group does?

Leadership and authority. How does the group handle issues of leadership and authority? Who leads formally? Informally? How? Is authority by position or by expertise and competence?

---

[2] Edgar H. Schein, *Process Consultation* (Reading, Mass.: Addison-Wesley, 1971), p. 9.

Intergroup cooperation and competition. How does the group work with other groups?

Conflict. How is conflict handled in the group? Constructively? Destructively? Is it ignored?

The PC approach to OD is designed to give the client (usually the manager) insight into what occurs around him and between him and others. The events and activities observed are those occurring between the manager and his work group in the normal flow of work, especially in managerial group meetings. Of particular importance are the manager's actions and their impact on those he works with.

The PC consultant meets with the managerial group while they are at work — that is, in a normal task meeting. The consultant observes them paying particular attention to the critical processes named above. He collects data primarily by direct observation, although he may also ask organization members, by either interview or questionnaire, for their views of these processes. Afterward, the consultant shares his observations with the manager and the work group.

The consultants' purpose in PC is threefold. His first aim is to make the client group aware of the processes they use to accomplish their work, to show *how* they work. The second is to make the client aware of the consequences of these key processes for the group's work, to show the ways in which *how* they work affects *what* they do. His third goal is to present the client with alternative processes, new ways of doing the work, which the group may choose to try.

At first glance, PC may seem a very simplistic approach to OD. Managers may resist the notion that they need someone to watch their groups work and then to tell them how they do it. Managers who have used the PC approach report they held similar attitudes at the outset, but their final opinions are quite different. As one manager said, "Using PC was like holding a mirror up to the group. For the first time we were able to see *how* we were working and the effects on *what* we were doing. I didn't like what I saw in me, especially the way my behavior affected others' communication. PC showed us some new ways to work. We like what we see in the mirror a whole lot better now, and the company is doing better too!"

Whether PC is really simple, or not as easy as it looks, it obviously works for some managers. The PC case illustration below will clarify just how the approach works and will help managers decide whether it will work for them.

A Process Consultation OD Case

The Lubo Company manufactures specialty clocks and has done so successfully for 14 years. It is a relatively small concern employing about 225 people in a single manufacturing facility. Sales have stabilized over the last four years in the range of $8-9 million. The company is managed by Frank Lubo, founder and principal owner. Frank's top management group consists of himself, the vice-presidents of finance and accounting, marketing, manufacturing, sales and distribution, and the newly appointed director of development. For the last two-and-a-half years Frank has been relatively inactive in the management of the company. With the development of a standardized product line and the stabilization of sales, he felt less need for his immediate involvement and began to devote most of his energy to community activities. He perceived his management group as a highly effective interdisciplinary team and assumed they would continue to perform without his riding herd on them.

The company performed according to plan for the first two years of this arrangement. Then, six months before the opening of this case, changes began to occur. First, Frank saw a need for a new product line – specifically, a compact digital clock with luminescent numerals. Frank appointed Carl Colbert to oversee the development of the prototype and to conduct the necessary feasibility and marketing studies. Carl had been assistant to the marketing vice-president as director of development and now was to join the management group, who were constituted as a project team to guide and oversee development of the "Lumino," as the new clock was named. The group was given three months from the completion of the prototype to the final go or no-go decision. It was anticipated that the total process would not exceed six months.

Three months passed and the Lumino prototype was not completed. Carl, when Frank confronted him, claimed the problems were managerial, not technological. When Frank met with the management group his observations confirmed Carl's claim. He found a lack of cooperation and conflicting, often incomplete information among top management regarding the "Lumino" project. As Frank expressed it, "It was as if they're all working on a different project! I had five people on a team and no two of them were playing the same game. I gave them three months to get it together. I wanted to know if the Lumino would work!"

There was little improvement in the ensuing three months. A prototype Lumino was constructed and feasibility and test-market studies were begun, but the group had no conclusive results. Worse yet, evidence of ineffective management began to appear in the normal operations of the company. Frank Lubo, now very concerned about his top management group, asked for help.

In an attempt to diagnose the real problems within the Lubo management group, the consultant asked to sit in on its next work meeting, which was to be chaired by Frank Lubo. Notice of the consultant's attendance was sent to all involved. Beforehand, the consultant met briefly with each of the managers, as a means both of introducing himself and of becoming more fully acquainted with their respective roles in the organization. The agenda for the meeting was: (1) monthly activity reports, (2) Lumino project report, and (3) inventory planning.

The meeting began at 4 P.M. in the Lubo conference room. The names of the participants and the seating arrangement at the outset of the meeting are on the diagram below.

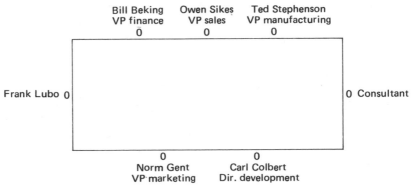

During this first meeting the consultant was interested primarily in observing communication among group members. As an aid to his direct observation he used the two simple observation forms, "who talks to whom" and "who talks, how often."

As the meeting progressed, some clear communication patterns emerged. During the monthly activity reports, in which each manager reported on the major activities of his area, the consultant observed that all the managers seemed to direct their reports to Owen Sikes, VP of sales and distribution. A few comments were directed to Lubo, but the majority of these came from Sikes. Of equal importance is that very few comments during this general information exchange were addressed to the total group. These observations were accumulated on the "who talks to whom" observational sheet, which, when completed for the initial agenda item, took the form reproduced in Figure 21. The reader may also see, as did the consultant, the inactivity of Carl Colbert during this period, the side conversation between Colbert and Gent, and Gent's direction of comments to Lubo. The "who talks to whom" form is a very simple but very informative aid in observing communication processes.

When discussion moved to reviewing progress on the Lumino project, Sikes and Colbert became the dominant contributors, each speaking often and at length. The other group members participated only sporadically. The frequency results reported on the "who talks, how often" form in Figure 22 picture what the consultant observed.

Figure 21. Who talks to whom? (Lubo meeting No. 1)

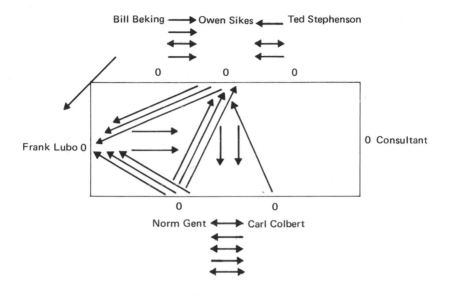

Figure 22. Who talks, how often? (Lubo meeting No. 2)

Agenda item: Lumino Project

Frank Lubo ——|————|—|——|—
Bill Beking —|——|
Owen Sikes ————|——————|————|—————————|————|
Ted Stephenson ——|—|—|
Carl Colbert ————————|————|—————|—————|——————|
Norm Gent —|—|—|——

(Note: Each dash represents approximately one minute of input by the designated individual. Each vertical bar represents the conclusion of a specific input.)

While the consultant was primarily interested in observing the management group's communication during this initial meeting, certain other processes were evident and are implied, if not directly illustrated, by the communication data. The informal leader was clearly Owen Sikes. The others directed their reports and comments to him and relied upon him to transmit them to Lubo. Apparently, Sikes' leadership came from others' perception of his ready access to Lubo. Gent was less inclined to direct his comments to Lubo through Sikes. The conflict over Lumino was between Sikes and Colbert. As they fought, the others either fled the conflict entirely (see Beking's frequency), or took supportive seconding roles on either side. Throughout the meeting, Frank Lubo's presence seemed to have very little effect upon the group. Nor did Frank attempt to affect the group's normal work patterns. This, too, is substantiated by the recorded observation of communication.

Other key processes were in play at this first meeting, of course, but the evidence of their effect was inconclusive. Later observations would reveal more about member roles and functions and group problem solving and decision making. From this observation of communication processes there was ample data to provide the management group with a mirror of its behavior.

At the conclusion of the business meeting the consultant presented his observations. First, he showed the group how they communicated with each other, duplicating and sharing with the group Figures 21 and 22. He discussed what he had been looking at and what he had seen in the group, drawing attention to specific examples. Confronted with a picture of its behavior, the group on its own began to identify consequences of the way the members communicate. This was done very cautiously. Some obvious points were not mentioned directly by the group, perhaps because they were felt to be too risky. Among the consequences implied but left unsaid were:

1. The management group does not consider Frank Lubo the operational leader of the company.
2. Owen Sikes is seen by most as the leader. Accordingly information flows to him, which enhances his leadership role.
3. Gent and Colbert do not recognize Sikes as the leader, do not treat him as such, and therefore are not privy to the information he has.
4. The conflict between Sikes and Colbert splits the group and to some degree scares them into inactivity.
5. These many sentiments are manifested in the way members of the group communicate with each other, which results in a lack of cooperation and lags in operational performance.

One would not expect a work group to come to such a critical self-assessment upon first examination of its communication patterns. Indeed, it was only much later in the Lubo PC OD program that some of these points emerged. At the first meeting the group, upon examining itself, was prepared to say that the lack of shared information caused by one-to-one versus one-to-all communication was a significant source of operational inefficiency and ineffectiveness.

This was an important admission for the group and led to corrective action to increase and improve group communication. The consultant presented a number of alternative techniques to the group, which selected a few to try out. The chairmanship of the top management meeting was rotated, written monthly activity reports were prepared for all and distributed prior to the meetings, and group sensing was used to elicit all members' opinions on agenda items. These techniques saw an improvement in the quantity and quality of top management communication, a change dramatically illustrated by Figure 23, which diagrams the discussion over a final decision on Lumino approximately three months (five meetings) after the initial PC meeting.

Figure 23. Who talks to whom? (Lubo meeting No. 6)

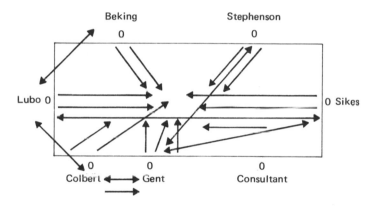

Continued PC work with Lubo Company eventually brought the group to a common awareness of the key process points identified earlier. Such an awareness was slow to evolve, but it did lead to major organizational changes. Frank Lubo reentered the organization actively and, together with his managers, became more attentive to the work processes of the group. The consultant no longer works with Lubo, but the PC OD effort continues. At each top management meeting the chairman appoints a process monitor whose job it is to comment at the conclusion of the meeting upon the effective and ineffective processes he observed. In addition, the management group continually experiments with alternative ways of working together. Throughout the PC OD effort Lubo has maintained its sales and profit position. The investment and improvement in key work processes have not been dramatically reflected on the balance sheet either positively or negatively, but they have been felt by all concerned.

The case of PC in the Lubo Company, incomplete as it may seem, is typical of PC OD efforts. Some PC consultants are more directive than others, some emphasize selected work processes, but their primary concerns are the same. There is always in PC an attempt to make the client aware of his behavior, aware of the consequences of his behavior, and aware of alternative ways of behaving. The work group and its work processes are observed and diagnosed in PC. Arousal of the group's awareness of its own processes and its introduction to alternatives constitute intervention in PC OD. Choosing whether to act upon this awareness of present and potential behaviors is the prerogative of the client.

Scoring Process Consultation OD

In terms of the critical choice criteria for managers, as the Lubo Company case clearly illustrates, PC is a relatively *unstructured* approach to OD. It is true that the consultant has in mind certain key dynamics and observational cues, but he has no control over the work processes he actually sees. The intervention in PC, like survey feedback, occurs when the consultant shares his observations. Unlike survey feedback, there is no predetermined plan for sharing the diagnosis in PC OD. This is a further demonstration of the *ad hoc* character of the PC approach.

The PC approach to OD views power as *shared* by all members of the work group. All members participate, either actively or passively, in the processes observed. All members should take responsibility for deciding whether or not the processes should be changed, and all members should participate in changing them. PC recognizes that the manager alone cannot change the work processes of the group. He can provide an important, indeed a necessary, model, but all members must share in the effort to change the processes of the total group.

Because PC OD focuses on the human interaction processes of the organization, the relationships that individuals develop in the work setting are important concerns. These *personal-work* relationships may be at the root of the communication, decision-making, or conflict disorders observed by the consultant. Where the focal group has a long work history prior to the PC effort, discussions of work processes often lead to an exploration of personal relationships within the work group. Some managers and groups find this element of PC threatening and attempt to escape the issues it raises through superficial treatment of the problem processes. This avoids probing sensitive personal-work relationships, but it also usually renders the PC effort ineffective. PC OD does not always deal directly with personal-work relationships, but the potential for such a focus is inherent in the approach.

While work processes are difficult to observe, they are even more difficult to make others aware of and still more difficult to change. With time, each of these tasks becomes easier, but managers should not underestimate the time required. PC is a relatively slow-paced *evolutionary* approach to OD. The consultant is usually present throughout this lengthy process, and skilled PC consultants are expensive. However, the real-time setting of PC means that opportunity costs are low. PC OD does not take the time and energy of key people away from operational concerns; it works as they work, where they work, on day-to-day affairs. Despite its slow pace and high consultant involvement, PC is a relatively *inexpensive* approach to OD because of its real-time orientation.

The initial stages of PC OD, like survey feedback, are *consultant centered.* The consultant selects from his many observations the two or three most critical work processes and directs the attention and energy of the work group to these. Ideally, as PC progresses, the work group develops the skills to carry out the program on its own. When this happens, the *client* takes control of PC. Most work groups remain highly dependent upon the consultant, and the ideal, client control, takes much time and effort to realize.

Since PC OD focuses on the processes of groups at work, it is natural to judge the effectiveness of PC OD by *process* criteria. Change in *how* a group works attests to the effectiveness of PC. Change in *what* the group does is assumed to follow, but product performance criteria are not applied to PC OD. At the best, data on the relationship between how groups work and what they produce are conflicting and inconclusive. Managers must judge for themselves and their people whether altered work processes will improve a group's output.

THE TEAM BUILDING APPROACH TO OD

Team building is the single most popular approach to OD used today. TB efforts can be found in organizations of every description, size, and locale from the U.S. Department of State to the local department store. Team building greatly resembles parts of both survey feedback and process consultation and is in fact a combination of these approaches to OD. By combining the simplicity of SF with the real-time relevance of PC, TB offers a very attractive program to managers considering OD. There is also some attraction in that the end product of TB, an effective "team," is something visible and meaningful to organization members who identify with effective teams in other contexts, such as sports and space exploration. This implicit symbolic value of the TB approach to OD should not be underestimated; it contributes greatly to the widespread acceptance of TB in organizations, but it may not convey accurately what TB involves.

Defining Team Building

Team building begins with the assumption that organizations do their work through a number of work teams of different kinds. The teams may be vertical slices of the organization, such as a functional group which includes the boss and all subordinates engaged in a particular area of work; these are called *family teams.* Or the teams may be composed of colleagues or peers, such as horizontal groupings of all the vice-presidents or all the regional sales managers; these are *cousin teams. Project teams* bring together organization members from a variety of functional areas to work on a specific activity. *Start-up teams* are often organized to initiate new activities or enterprises. These and countless other kinds of teams constitute the work groups of an organization. The TB approach to OD assumes that increasing the effectiveness of these teams will improve overall organizational performance.

TB is usually defined as a process of diagnosing and improving the effectiveness of a work group with particular attention to work procedures and interpersonal relationships within it, especially the role of the leader in relation to other group members. The TB approach is concerned with both the team's task procedures and the human processes encountered. These human processes are most important where they involve the team leader, who is most often the manager.

The specific agenda of a TB effort depends on the nature of the team — whether it is a new team, a functional team, or a project team — and the choices made by the particular consultant involved. Most often, the pattern followed is similar to that in survey feedback. An off-site setting away from the day-to-day pressures of the work place is secured for three to five days. Prior to the meeting, the consultant interviews team members individually to collect data on the team's task and process objectives.

The meeting begins by setting an agenda assigning an order of priority to the topics and issues developed by the interviews. The consultant's role is to help members air the personal and interpersonal issues that stand in the way of task performance. The climate must be a candid one seeking and encouraging open expression of feelings and opinions about the many forces affecting the work of the team. Because many of the issues raised will center on the team leader/manager, special effort must be made to ensure that he "hears" the team members' concerns and that these are expressed in a constructive manner. Action steps are chosen and members' responsibilities assigned before the meeting ends. Follow-through steps are developed to ensure that action is taken and that the spirit of the team meeting is maintained. This description of TB comes to life in the following brief case.

A Team Building OD Case

Georgette Bobick is vice-president of human resource development (HRD) for a major national restaurant chain. Reporting to Bobick are Jim Dent, division head (DH) of employee relations; Phil Gish, DH of recruitment and placement; Pete Barker, DH of compensation; and Verna Molter, DH of training. Together this group constitutes the HRD management team and is responsible for the personnel functions of the company. Relations among the members of the team have been deteriorating for some time because of a growing "each to his own" atmosphere which alienated the members from each other. For a time this distance did not impede their effectiveness, but recent efforts to build separate empires have resulted in conflicts at the branch level. Branch restaurant managers have reported to the president that the conflicting communications and activities of the HRD divisions were at best neutralizing one another, and at worst creating confusion at the "store" level. The president immediately went to Bobick and told her to "get her people together and get them together fast."

Bobick first took internal steps to renew the team spirit. She saw the problem as a lack of shared information. To remedy this, she changed team meetings from monthly to weekly and established that all communications from a division head to the branches had to be aired first at a meeting of division heads. Branch managers were to be brought to headquarters to resolve difficult problems, rather than having division heads visit branches. In short, Bobick's means of getting her people together was to make the work of any one division head the work of all division heads.

The results of this first internal team building effort were predictable. The attempt to communicate to the branches with one voice failed. Weekly meetings were attended grudgingly, if at all. Division heads usually sent a subordinate rather than appear themselves. Communication with the branches ceased entirely because of the difficulty of obtaining the required clearance at the division heads' meetings. The sheer logistics of bringing branch managers to headquarters to resolve difficult problems mitigated against frequent visits, and interaction between the branches and headquarters deteriorated further. Now watching Bobick and the HRD group closely, the president was quick to see how poorly these initial team-building efforts were proceeding, and at a second meeting with Bobick directed her to seek external help. Bobick agreed that she needed help and contracted with an external consultant to provide the team building assistance the HRD group needed.

The consultant began by individually interviewing each of the members of the team, using the "diagnostic que-sort" as an interviewing aid. The que-sort enabled the consultant to classify team members' observations into four team concerns: goals, the structure of work, work processes, and interpersonal processes. From this diagnostic effort, the consultant concluded that goals were not a major area of concern to the members of the HRD unit—in fact, there was considerable agreement over the services HRD was to provide to the rest of the company. However, there was considerable disagreement over the best way to provide these services, the question of who was to do what and when, and the way the members should work together to provide the services. Team members did not express great concern about interpersonal processes and relations. There was a general feeling that if the structure of the work and the actual work processes could be smoothed out, the interpersonal relations among team members would improve.

With this information, the consultant designed a three-day team building workshop for the members of the HRD unit. The workshop design allowed time to be allocated to activities most appropriate to the areas presenting problems to the HRD team. While the program illustrated here was designed for the HRD team, a similar program could be used for other teams in other organizations with time allocations appropriate for the problems they face.

The HRD team building workshop began with a brief discussion of the theory of teams in organizations and the consultant's view of teams and their roles in organizations. The participants were invited to share their views of the role of teams in this company and their experiences with teams here and in other companies. Discussion began on a theoretical plane, but the team members warmed to the subject as they discussed their experiences with teams in other companies and their views on the potential role of teams in the HRD division.

From the discussion emerged general agreement that teams were important in the effective functioning of HRD within the company. Related to the role of teams was the importance of respecting the need for individual acts within the team. Team members strongly insisted that not all of their work could be done in teams, that not all of it needed team approval before being carried out. In their minds, an effective team was one in which there was sufficient agreement about what was to be done and how it was to be done to leave individual members free to do their work without constant reference back to the team.

These important ideas about the meaning of teams to the people of HRD were written out on newsprint and put up on the wall around the workshop room. In later discussions during the three days, these ideas became important reference points to remind team members what kind of team they were trying to build in HRD.

After the initial discussion, the consultant presented to the participants the data from the interviews. Interview responses were first grouped into the four categories: goals, the structure of work, work processes, and interpersonal relations. Observations that appeared frequently were noted, but at no point was any individual singled out as being responsible for a particular observation or comment. The participants were encouraged to acknowledge responses they had made during the interview, and several did. As might have been expected, Bobick was the target of many critical remarks during the interviews and much of this criticism again surfaced in the workshop.

The consultant was careful to keep review of the data at the level of shared information and views and to avoid interpersonal confrontation and personal innuendo that could destroy any later effort at real team building. With the consultant's guidance, the participants of the HRD team were able to find two areas of general agreement and two areas of great concern. Again, the areas of agreement were goals and interpersonal relations, and the areas of dissatisfaction were the structure of work and work processes. Discussion moved quickly from the review of the data to using it in setting an agenda for the remaining time in the team-building workshop.

In setting the agenda, the group thought it best to discuss team goals first, even though there was general agreement about them, in order to clarify understandings of the relationship of HRD goals and priorities to those of individual team members and those of the company. The group decided that half a day would be adequate for this. It wanted to spend two days of the three-day workshop on the two most critical areas of concern; the structure of work and work processes. The remaining half day was to be devoted to dealing with interpersonal processes initiated during the team building workshop or left over from prior working relationships and to the development of action agendas. The consultant insisted that the group make a commitment to future team and individual actions before leaving the workshop. Agreement on this general allocation of time was reached and work began.

As the group opened its discussion of team goals, two questions became central: What does the company think we are about? What are we, in fact, about? Georgette Bobick, as spokesperson for the company, was put on the spot to define for the group HRD's responsibilities. Bobick had brought with her several documents from the president and other staff executives describing in broadest terms the role of HRD within the company. The group was pleased to have the importance of HRD in the company's operation and future plans reaffirmed, but they were disappointed that the president was so vague in detailing HRD's responsibilities. Bobick interpreted the breadth of the president's statements of HRD goals as respect for the expertise of the members of the team; the team, on the other hand, interpreted his lack of detail as lack of understanding of HRD's precise role and contributions. Team members began to express their views of how their activities contributed to the broad goals of HRD and the company.

During this discussion a collaborative spirit developed as team members began to help each other describe how their specific functions contributed to the overall work of HRD and how that in turn contributed to the effective functioning of the company. The consultant guided the discussion to a statement of the general goals of the department and the contributing goals of each of the member divisions. These goals were recorded on newsprint and put up around the walls of the room alongside the notes about the meaning of teams. Seeing their work in black and white gave the team members a sense of achievement and a sense of progress. There was a discernible atmosphere of collaboration and comradeship, the first that had been evident in the team in many months, as the members were quick to observe. The consultant urged team members to be mindful of their sense of collaboration and comradeship as they pursued more difficult and perhaps more competitive discussions about the structure of work and work processes.

To open the TB session on the structure of work, the consultant presented his conception of the purpose of that session: to clarify understanding of who on the team is to do what and when. Three devices were used to focus the discussion of team members. First the members were asked to draw organizational pictures of how they got work done in the human resource development department. These informal personal organization charts gave a quick picture of the actual flow of work in HRD. It was clear that the manner in which work was actually done was quite different from a formal organization chart's description of the way work ought to be done. Some members of the team seemed to be involved in every activity within the department; others were involved in little outside their own efforts, and within these, they were completely autonomous. These representations of the structure of work led to a discussion of team-versus-individual issues.

The consultant next asked members of the team to draw up a list of problems they felt to be team problems falling within the province of all participants. They were asked to draw up a second list of the problems which they felt to be individual problems and of concern only to themselves. This was an important task for the team members because it represented the first step toward putting their own concept of an effective team into operation—that is, it was their first effort toward building a team in which members would be free to pursue certain individual activities without prior approval by other team members. When the lists were completed, roughly one-third of the problems fell into the team-problem category. The remainder were seen as in the province of the individual division heads within HRD.

The completion of this step led to a third, the preparation of an "involvement-input-information profile." Each member was asked to put the team problems into three categories. The first category, involvement, contained problems the team member felt he or she must be personally involved in solving. The second category, input, included those problems about which the team member had important information that ought to be considered before a decision was reached but which did not require him or her to be personally involved in solving. Into the third category, interest, went problems the team member wanted to be aware of but did not need to be involved in solving. This activity allowed the members of the team to sort out their work and to identify for any given issue the individuals who ought to be involved in decision making, the team participants who had information that should be considered, and those who were merely interested.

The discussion during this process was long and heated, but ultimately very helpful. Some members were thought to be "copping out" of responsibility by not labeling certain problems as ones they should be involved in. Other members were accused of being busybodies because of their desire to be involved in everything. Each individual was asked to give reasons for his or her categorization of the team problems. Through this discussion and explanation, team members developed a real appreciation for the specific details of each other's work and for the interrelationships among divisional tasks.

Again with the consultant's guidance, the group moved toward consensus on an involvement-input-interest profile for each team problem. The group suggested color coding communications to conform to the profile categories—blue sheets for involvement communications, green for input communications, and pink for interest communications. They agreed to experiment with this structure in their work for a three-month period, after which they would review their own personal involvement-input-interest profiles and those developed for the team as a whole.

This full day on restructuring their work was the most difficult of the three days for the group, but it was also the most rewarding. Ultimately it would have the most lasting effect on their efforts. From the structure of work the team moved on to consideration of their work processes.

The consultant had asked Georgette Bobick to bring with her several problems that the team needed to work on, actual operating issues that needed decisions and action. The session on work processes began with the consultant inviting the team to tackle these problems. Under Bobick's leadership the team began to work on the first problem on the agenda, one involving cutbacks in the labor force. The consultant observed the team at work using many of the diagnostic aids discussed in the preceding section on process consultation. The session was also videotaped for later replay.

Particularly evident during the group's work were poor communication and inadequate decision-making processes. At the conclusion of the group's deliberations on the initial problem, the consultant replayed the videotape and led the group through an analysis of their own techniques. The communication and decision-making weaknesses were as evident to the members of the group as they had been to the consultant. They realized that the way they had tried to communicate and make decisions was ineffective; it resulted in both a waste of time and considerable confusion over what action they had committed themselves to. But they were at a loss for alternatives.

The consultant presented them with different group meeting techniques, different ways to make decisions, and different methods for sharing information within a group. Again following the pattern of process consultation, he gave the group three simulated problem-solving tasks in increasing order of difficulty and invited them to experiment with new communication and decision-making styles in their attempts to solve these problems. The tasks were fun and involving, and they provided a relatively low-risk atmosphere in which individual members could experiment with new behaviors. The group was again invited to view a videotape of their work on the simulated tasks, and to pay particular attention to the consequences of their experiments in new behaviors.

Following the second videotape replay, the group was asked to work on the remaining problems brought in by Bobick. The consultant did not admonish the members to experiment with new behaviors in this real-time context; rather, they were left to decide for themselves which behavior would be most appropriate and effective. For the most part, the group was very good about trying newly learned communication and decision-making behaviors, and they felt a sense of achievement when these efforts proved to be successful.

As time for the resolution of the remaining problems grew short, the team members began to fall back into their old established ways of sharing information and making decisions about the information they had shared. The consultant intervened to point this out, and also to point out that the team shouldn't expect to completely integrate new patterns of behavior overnight and apply them with full success. Nonetheless, team members were disappointed by their performance under the pressure of time and committed themselves to further work on their group processes in the future.

During the final half-day of the workshop, team members decided to concentrate on developing an understanding of their personal interaction as a variable in team performance. They began with a general discussion of individual members' personal styles of working in the team throughout the preceding two-and-a-half days. The consultant invited team members to negotiate around personal styles and around behavior in the work team. This was done through a role negotiation exercise. Each individual was asked to take a sheet of the large newsprint and to record on it his name and three columns, one headed "more," one "less," and one "stop/start." These sheets were then put up on the walls.

The members were encouraged to go to the sheet of every other member and write in the "more" category the team behaviors they would like to see more of, in the "less" category those they would like to see less of, and in the "stop/start" category the ones they would like to see that person either stop or start. Members were then encouraged to negotiate their lists on a *quid pro quo* basis: Georgette Bobick might start doing more of a behavior to please Jim Dent if in exchange Dent would do less of a behavior that Bobick wants decreased. No one was required to negotiate anything if in their opinion a fair exchange could not be made.

This role negotiation provided members with a framework for settling difficult behavioral conflicts that had emerged either during the three-day team building workshop or in their prior work experience. The negotiation was spirited and well received. Further, it led to commitments from each person to every other person in the team to adopt or end certain behaviors which all felt would contribute to more effective team performance.

These commitments culminated in the action agendas, statements of a future course of personal action written by each individual. The statement followed a common format answering five questions: What will you do? How will you do it? Who else does it involve? When will it be done? How will you know when it's done? Each action agenda was then shown to every other member of the team and deposited with the consultant for return to the team member, at the end of six weeks, as a direct reminder of the course of action committed to and as an indirect reminder of the kinds of general behavior commitments made during the team building session.

The three days ended with a general feeling of satisfaction with the work that had been done and a common grasp of the work that remained to be done. Team members felt that one three-day meeting was not at all adequate, that it was a good start, but that it was far from getting them all the way to where they wanted to be. An additional meeting as soon as possible was requested. In fact, three days off-site are a bare minimum for effective team building. Most programs work much longer, from five to seven days. Team building efforts usually follow off-site programs with on-site work and a continuing relationship between the consultant and the team. This was the case in Bobick's department, and the effort is still underway.

In this description of the team building process special attention should be given to the unique position of the manager or team leader. Many authors have written at length about team management and the skills necessary for its effective practice. Team management requires different skills from the more commonplace patterns of management—such as one-to-one, boss/subordinate relationships, or group situations in which authority is vested completely in a single leader. The skills of team management, delegation, shared power and responsibility, trust, and open communication have to be learned, and team building is often the first learning laboratory for the team manager. Thus the leader (in this case Georgette Bobick) and her skills and relations with the others often become the central focus of team building efforts.

William Crockett participated as a leader in a team building effort in the U.S. Department of State. In reflecting on his participation he portrays with insight the leader's role and attendant anxieties in team building, particularly the risks of exposing himself and his opinions of his staff to the team and the problems of sharing responsibility. Crockett wonders, as many leaders do, if it wouldn't be easier, simpler, and better for him to direct things to be done since he has the authority to do so.[3]

The peculiar role of the team leader in team building efforts does much to shape the process. The consultant spends considerable time with the leader before and during the team building effort to prepare him for the confrontation and communication that are required to make team building effective. The entire team building approach is attuned to the needs and skills of the leader—the process moves as quickly or as slowly as he moves. In effect, in team building the leader/manager places his fortunes with his people in the hands of the consultant, and it is of critical importance that he choose the consultant wisely.

The Bobick-HRD case reflects team building as it is pursued in an existing continuing team that has problems. Team building may also be used to develop a new team, one which has no problems and has yet to begin to work together. The basic areas of consideration remain the same: team goals, the structure of work, work processes, and intergroup relationships. Obviously, the tenor of discussions of these topics is often very different in the new team, with far more time spent deliberating team goals and the relationship between individual effort and team goals. Work processes need to be designed, rather than redesigned, and often problems with the structure of work have yet to be experienced. New team discussions of interpersonal relations are much more tentative, for members have had little exposure to each other and little time to adapt to each other's styles of behavior.

These differences notwithstanding, the general outline of team concerns presented in the Bobick case provides an effective standard framework for working out the problems of any team, whether new or existing, whether composed of members of a specific functional department or of peers from several departments. The team's makeup may differ, but its context is much the same. That context can best be defined in relation to other OD contexts by measuring team building against managers' critical choice criteria.

---

[3]W. J. Crockett, "Team Building: One Approach to OD," *Journal of Applied Behavioral Science,* May–June 1970, pp. 291–306.

Scoring Team Building OD

One of the popular advantages of the team building approach to OD over process consultation lies in its more structured format. It usually examines the four basic areas of team behavior (goals, the structure of work, work processes, and interpersonal relations), which remain constant from one type of team to another. However, as the Bobick case illustrates, the allocation of time in a team building effort corresponds to the specific needs of the team and, in fact, changes throughout the team building effort as these needs change. For this reason team building is actually *sequentially structured* and falls between the structured survey feedback methods and the relatively unstructured process consultation approaches to OD. Thus team building meets the needs of groups and organizations who rebel against the rigidity of the structure provided by survey feedback and those who dislike the lack of structure and apparent lack of direction in process consultation. Certainly its sequentially structured plan is one of the properties which has made team building so popular among managers today.

A second reason for the popularity of TB is that it poses no threat to traditional assumptions about power. It assumes that *power is unilateral,* that the manager has initial authority and ultimate responsibility. The prerogative to share or not to share that authority with the group as the intervention ensues rests entirely with the manager. Here again we see the critical role of the manager or team leader in setting the direction and tone of the team building process.

Team building, like process consultation, focuses on the human interaction processes of the organization in terms of the relationships among individuals in the work setting. While team building offers the opportunity to move into the arena of interpersonal relationships in more depth than does process consultation, few team building efforts take advantage of this opportunity until they are well along.

This implied change in the character of team building OD efforts implies their slow pace. A single TB meeting or even a brief series of meetings, regardless of how intense, seldom brings discernible changes in organizational performance. Team changes come with time and a persistent commitment to experimenting with new team behaviors. Success in their new behaviors encourages team members to try new experiments. The successes build on each other and changes in behavior of individual members of the team, and of the team as a whole, occur with increasing speed. We therefore speak of the pace of the team building approach to OD as being *incremental* in character.

Team building OD takes key organization people away from their operational concerns. True, during the off-site time members are at work on back-home problems, but they are not available to interact with their organization associates, and much of their time is spent in developing and experimenting with skills which may appear to be only indirectly related to the performance of their function in the organization. The opportunity cost of team building thus is, at a minimum, moderate. Added to this is the cost of "hands-on" consultant time during the off-site period and back home in the organization as the team continues its work and experiments with new team behaviors. This high opportunity cost and need for continuing consultancy combine to make team building a *moderately expensive* approach to OD.

Like process consultation, again, team building in its initial phases is highly dependent for success on the role of the consultant, on his diagnosis of critical team concerns, and on the alternatives that he presents to the team. The consultant's initial direction of the group makes the difference between effective and ineffective team building. As the process proceeds, however, the client should take control. The client should develop the skill to diagnose inefficiencies and ineffectiveness in team behaviors and should also develop behavioral alternatives for the team to explore as means to more effective performance.

Thus the professional relationship in team building OD efforts is a *dual* one, with responsibility shared by both the consultant and the client or client group. However, in team building, client groups seem better able to break away from dependency on the consultant than in process consultation. They more quickly identify problem behaviors and the means for resolving these problems, perhaps because of the attention to goals and the structure of work which is such an important part of the team building process but which is left out of process consultation methods.

This attention to goals and the structure of work also makes team building effectiveness most properly judged by both *process and product criteria.* As the Bobick case clearly illustrated, change in the *how* of a group's work is an important part of team building which emerges for the most part from process consultation. Team building is also concerned with changing *what* the group does. Goals and the structure of work are the critical elements in doing this. As a result, at the conclusion of team building, the client team should work more efficiently and effectively, and a consultant can expect to be held accountable for improving the group's processes and products.

The addition of attention to the goals of the work team and how the team structures its work to achieve its goals distinguishes team building from process consultation. This distinction makes team building seem less "soft" to managers, and therefore more appealing, as they make critical choices of how to invest their scarce development dollars.

THE LABORATORY TRAINING APPROACH TO OD

Team building may be the most popular of contemporary approaches to OD, but for many years the laboratory training or T-group approach to OD received the most press coverage. No single strategy for organizational change has received more attention, and no strategy has contributed more to the confusion that surrounds OD and its meaning for managers.

In objective retrospect, it now appears that the laboratory approach to OD was a fad of the 1960s and not a lasting organizational phenomenon. During that period several industrial giants, notably those in the aerospace industry, enthusiastically adopted sensitivity (or laboratory) training as an approach for improving organizational effectiveness. This was viewed by others as an outright endorsement of the laboratory training approach to OD, which understandably led to further adoptions.

These uses of T-groups in the business community were seen as so revolutionary a move that they were covered by both the popular business press and academic publications. This attention in turn led to the popular identification of sensitivity training as the sole approach to organization development and to the definition of organization development as sensitivity training in organizations. Actual use of T-groups in organizations has decreased so drastically that the author is aware of no business organization presently using this OD approach exclusively. Yet the definition of OD as laboratory training lives on for many managers.

For this reason it is important that the essentials of the laboratory training (or sensitivity training or T-group or human relations training) approach to OD are clarified for managers.

Defining Laboratory Training

The fundamental assumption of the laboratory training approach to OD is that organizational effectiveness is a function of the individuals' values, attitudes, and behavioral styles, and that, consequently, problems of organizational performance are problems of improper attitudes and improper behaviors of members of the organization. It follows from this assumption that the way to enhance organizational performance and thereby increase effectiveness is to develop values, attitudes, and behavioral styles conducive to more effective performance. What the laboratory approach attempts to do is to create a particular kind of social climate, or order, and to give individuals an opportunity to experience and experiment with the skills appropriate to that order — in other words, it sets out to create a human laboratory in which old attitudes and behaviors can be examined and new ones tried.

One consultant familiar with the laboratory approach gives the following explanation of it: The typical laboratory design attempts to create a temporary environment to generate learning which can be applied at the work site. Activities within this laboratory environment emphasize that certain norms or values can improve interpersonal and intergroup relations while helping meet important personal and organizational needs at the same time. Participants gain experience with attitudes and behavioral skills necessary to approach these norms. Organization members become convinced that laboratory norms should guide behavior in organizations and that they can provide or develop attitudes and behavioral skills appropriate to these norms.[4]

The climate sought in laboratory training is characterized by the following norms or values in the work setting.

1. Complete and free communication should take place within, between, and across hierarchical levels of the organization. Patterns of communication should be allowed to develop in response to the communication needs of members of the organization, rather than in response to artificially structured separations between superiors and subordinates or employees and managers.

2. In managing conflict, the organization should rely upon consensus, as opposed to coercion or imposed compromise. All parties involved in organizational conflicts should also be involved in the resolution of the conflicts, and the resolution should be produced through mutual input and exchange rather than through domination by one party or imposition on both parties of a compromise settlement with which neither is satisfied.

3. Organizational influence should be based on the competence of individual members rather than on their formal positions or personal whims. Decisions ought to be made by those most qualified to decide, without regard to their position or level in the organizational hierarchy, or to their personal charm or charisma.

4. Organizations ought to respect norms that permit the expression of emotional as well as task-oriented behavior. Management should not exclude the emotional content and tone of member behaviors from organizational situations but, rather, should allow free expression within the organizational situation.

5. Organizations ought to accept conflict as a natural occurence to be dealt with willingly and openly. Avoiding conflict and pretending that it does not exist are dysfunctional for individual and organizational performance.

While many managers agree with the norms the laboratory approach seeks to create, all managers recognize that these are quite different from the rules

---

[4] Robert T. Golembiewski and Stokes B. Carrigan, "Planned Change in Organization Style Based on the Laboratory Approach," *Administrative Science Quarterly*, January–February 1970, p. 79.

of behavior in most organizations. Managers have been quick to point out that they fly in the face of organizational tradition and the habits of organization members. In addition, behavior in accordance with these norms can be frustrating and dysfunctional for members of an organization which does not subscribe to these rules of behavior.

Both of these points address the critical problem in the laboratory approach to OD: the transfer of learning to the work situation. This transfer problem becomes all the more evident as attention turns from the objectives of the laboratory approach to OD, as stated above, to the actual laboratory approach processes and procedures illustrated below.

A Laboratory Training OD Case

Approaches to OD discussed previously were illustrated by cases clarifying the execution of the approach. This is not possible here, for even a brief case history of the laboratory approach in an organization would extend far beyond the scope of this survey. Also, descriptions of what actually occurs in a T-group OD effort tend to be illusive and often cloud rather than clarify the essential operating elements. The following general description of sensitivity training in organizations was distilled from several case histories. It is admittedly superficial, but it is entirely sufficient for our purposes.

Sensitivity training in an organization is usually undertaken after diagnosis reveals that significant organizational problems stem from individuals' values and behaviors manifested in specific interpersonal relationships. The participating parties are brought together to work in small groups over an extended period of time. They learn through examining their own experiences, their feelings, their reactions to others, their observations, and their behavior. The time spent in these groups varies, depending on the size of the group, the intensity of its work, and the specific design of the laboratory, but most groups meet for a total of 20 to 40 hours. This time may be in solid blocks of one or two eight-hour days, in a one- or two-week residential program, or spread out over several weekends or months.

The laboratory itself is a relatively unstructured environment. That is, it proceeds without clearly defined predetermined goals, rules, procedures, agendas, or member roles. The participants establish these in the laboratory to meet their own needs. The consultant plays a facilitating rather than a traditional leading role. It is his job to set a climate emphasizing trust and decreasing risk among the participants. He intends it to be a climate in which individuals feel free to relax their attachment to old values, attitudes, and behavioral skills, and to experiment with and evaluate new ones.

The focus of the laboratory is on personal and interpersonal data produced by the behavior of members within the laboratory setting. Thus the participants' learning consists of the data revealed by their behavior in the group. T-group settings are usually highly charged emotionally, with members becoming intensely and intimately involved with one another and reporting that the experience had significant impact on them personally. A major question remains regarding the impact of laboratory experiences on organizations.

The laboratory method is now 30 years old. Our experience with it in and out of organizations over these years has not gone unexamined. The laboratory training approach to OD has been the subject of more research, attention, discussion, and debate than any other approach to OD, and yet what we know of its effects is very little. Sparse though it may be, our knowledge of the usual effects of the laboratory approach to OD is very important to managers.

Four major changes seem to occur *for individuals* as a result of the laboratory experience:

1. They experience a reduction in extreme behaviors and a tendency toward the "norm."
2. They become more self-aware and more self-disclosing.
3. They improve their listening and participative skills.
4. They develop new perspectives on their environments.

These are predictable and significant experiences for individuals, but the manager must ask how they will enhance organizational performance. How is individual learning to be transferred to the organizational setting? This question is the Achilles heel of the laboratory approach to OD.

Scoring the Laboratory Training Approach to OD

The crucial issue in programs based on the laboratory approach to OD is the ability of participants to transfer into an organizational context their highly personal experience with norms, attitudes, and behavioral skills in a laboratory small-group setting. In many respects, the nature of the lab approach does not facilitate this transfer. In almost every one of the dimensions of OD that are critical to managers, the laboratory approach is at odds with what we know of the traditional functions of organizations.

Perhaps the overriding characteristic of the laboratory approach is its extremely unstructured nature. There is no predetermined plan during either the diagnostic phase or any subsequent intervention. Neither the consultant nor members of the client group know from one moment to the next what is going to happen or how the events taking place will ultimately affect their performance and the performance of the organization. The absence of rigidly structured plans can often spur creative interaction and encourage innovative ideas, but the ambiguity of a completely unstructured approach can just as often be a source of tremendous personal frustration and anxiety. Where there is a great amount of emotional tension, the likelihood increases that the lack of structure will lead to frustration rather than to functional creativity.

Decisions in the laboratory approach to OD are shared by the group. As in the case of team building, this sharing of power is often not initially the case, but it develops as the group proceeds. The leader of the work group becomes a focal point for discussions of power. Because of the intensely personal character of data generated in laboratory training, it is extremely important that in using this approach to OD the leader be both personally and interpersonally strong and competent.

Obviously, personal relationships and styles are the core of the laboratory approach to OD, for it assumes that personal values and behaviors not only lie at the heart of organizational problems but also identify the boundaries of the search for organizational solutions.

This intense focus on personal values and behaviors largely accounts for the relatively slow pace of the laboratory approach to OD. During the actual training sessions change takes place very quickly as individuals react to old behaviors and experiment with new ones. However, the transfer of these new behaviors, first to the work place and then throughout the work place, is a very slow, evolutionary process.

Because the laboratory training approach to OD requires the participants to invest intensive periods of time, the opportunity costs of such a program are very high. Mention should also be made of the psychological costs of creating a climate in which participants feel free to examine old values and behaviors and experiment with new ones. This behavior in itself carries high personal risk and requires considerable psychological investment by participants. Action in the face of this risk requires even greater effort.

These issues are magnified when laboratory training is taken into an organization as the exclusive method of OD, for despite the emphasis on making participation voluntary, few individuals may in fact voluntarily stay out of the program. The result is that many participants are in effect forced, at high personal cost, to examine and experiment with values and behaviors against their will. For these reasons of high opportunity costs and high psychological costs, the laboratory training approach to OD is the *most expensive* of those considered here.

The definition and description of the laboratory training approach to OD make it clear that what happens in the laboratory depends completely on what the participants make happen. The data generated from their own behavior is what participants learn. Thus in the laboratory training approach to OD the client is in total control of the OD program. When this type of *client control* is combined with the absence of structure, the laboratory training approach may appear to lack any control whatever over the process.

Finally, because the laboratory training approach to OD seeks to change the values and behaviors of individual participants, these must be examined to give a fair evaluation of the impact of this approach. Laboratory training OD assumes that more effective values and behaviors will lead to more effective organizational processes, the relationship is indirect, and change in personal values and attitudes may not be reflected in organizational processes. Managers evaluating the effects of the laboratory approach to OD should certainly not expect changes in production-related behaviors to indicate the effectiveness of the approach.

It may seem that this discussion of the laboratory training approach to OD has been less objective and, indeed, much harsher than discussions of other approaches. Given the nature of the laboratory approach, experience with its implementation, and its implications for organizations, such a strongly critical description is warranted. The personal readiness and interpersonal and psychological abilities required to render the laboratory training approach effective are not to be found in many individuals. There is a serious question as to whether or not such readiness and abilities are needed by most individuals in order for them to lead effective organizational lives. The major point is that a unique set of problems and unique personal qualities of organization members are required before the laboratory training approach to OD is either needed or can be used effectively. Since most managers have neither these kinds of problems nor such people, the laboratory training approach to OD should remain only a remote possibility.

THE PACKAGED PROGRAM APPROACH TO OD

Packaged program approaches to OD offer standardized formats and sets of procedures and fixed goals. Of the many approaches to OD, these are the most commercial. They are usually copyrighted and associated with and practiced only by the consultant or consultants who devised them or by the consultant's corporate representatives.

The Packaged Programs

Today there are a wide variety of such OD programs. Two of the more popular are Blake and Mouton's "Grid Organization Development" and Gordon Lippitt's "ITORP" (Implementing the Organization Renewal Process).[5]

[5] Robert R. Blake and Jane S. Mouton, *Building a Dynamic Organization Through Grid Organization Development* (Reading, Mass.: Addison-Wesley, 1969). Gordon Lippitt, *Organization Renewal* (New York: Appleton-Century-Crofts, 1969).

Many managers may be aware of the availability of such programs through aggressive direct mail advertising, books written by consultants to sell their own programs, presentations at professional meetings, or acquaintance with managers, and there are many, who have successfully used a packaged program in their own organizations. Managers would probably not be aware of the availability of these programs through reading the literature on organization development, for in general, academics have either ignored the existence of commercial programs or attacked their suitability for organizations. The one exception to this general rule is the Blake and Mouton Grid Organization Development.

Grid Organization Development is the packaged program which comes most immediately to mind when one mentions commercial organizational change efforts. It is the best developed and articulated, the most extensively marketed and researched, and for these reasons, the most popular of the packaged programs. Because of its popularity and because it displays the major characteristics of all packaged programs, it is taken here as a convenient vehicle for examining the packaged program approach to OD in general.

An obvious feature distinguishing this from other approaches to OD is its highly commercialized nature, a distinction not to be set aside lightly. Well marketed and attractively packaged programs compete for the attention of the manager in terms that are familiar to him. A major advantage of packaged programs over alternative approaches to OD is their direct appeal to the particular concerns of managers. This commercial distinction, while significant, is ultimately less important for managers than are the distinctions in content and form.

The outstanding features of packaged programs are their rigid formats and procedures derived from preconceptions of how an organization should function. For example, the ITORP program focuses on 12 critical organizational renewal processes as levers for improving organizational effectiveness. In the more renowned Grid OD program, six phases of organization development and corporate excellence build on the basic concept of the "Managerial Grid,"® a descriptive graph illustrating variations in management styles according to the relative amounts of concern shown for people and for performance. For example, a 1–9 manager has a high concern for people but gives little attention to output, while a 9–1 manager is just the opposite.

The Grid OD program uses the basic concepts of the Grid to bring about total organizational effectiveness through a six-phase program:

Phase I. The managerial grid is used as a theoretical framework for understanding the behavioral dynamics of the corporation's culture.
Phase II. In settings of actual work, organization teamwork is examined and tested against the grid model for the perfection of problem-solving methods.

Phase III. Interaction between organized units of the company is considered at points where cooperation and coordination are vital to success.

Phase IV. The top management team studies the properties of an ideal strategic corporate model necessary to bring corporate profitability logic to a maximum thrust condition across all teams in the organization.

Phase V. Implements the conversion of the corporation team from what it has been to what it will become under the ideal strategic corporate model.

Phase VI. Measures changes in conditions from pre-Phase I to post-Phase V.

In theory, this strategy takes three to five years to be wholly implemented. The point here is not so much what is done in the Grid OD effort as how it is done. In this regard, several components of the Grid program should be noted. It is a comprehensive and well-articulated strategy for moving an organization to a presupposed ideal end state. Blake and Mouton, like the authors of other packaged programs, have a distinct idea of what an organization should be like and what behaviors should characterize the activities of its members. Toward this end the Grid program is organized into sequential phases, each with distinct activities and goals leading to the desired end state. There is great reliance on prepackaged, standardized, instrumented techniques: prescribed events and exercises, including paper and pencil attitudinal measurements that serve both diagnostic and intervention purposes shaping the direction and development of the group and its participants.

The packaged program approach begins by training top management in the values and application of the program, then moves downward through all the levels of the organization. Final evaluation of the packaged program is an internal function of the package itself. From the point of initial diagnosis onward, progress is measured in terms of progress toward the desired goal state. These observations regarding the general properties of packaged programs, based on those of the Grid OD program, may become clearer when we look at a brief illustrative case of the Managerial Grid OD program.

A Grid Approach Case

SBM is a major marketing firm in one of the developing Southwestern markets. Despite the rapid growth of this market in the last five years, SBM has consistently fallen behind its competitors in both the number of its accounts and its total billing. In an effort to turn SBM around, the East Coast parent company assigned a new directing manager to the SBM office. He immediately set out to establish a new administrative group and to assess the situation at the firm. To centralize control, he created to assist him an office of the manager with two new staff members and one present staff member. The first task of the newly formed manager's office was to plan SBM's turn-around program. Review of the firm's performance in the recent past defined three immediate tasks for the manager's office: (1) improving financial planning, (2) increasing staff capabilities, and (3) developing a new SBM organizational plan overcoming short-term weaknesses in financial planning and staff capabilities.

In the new manager's view, the staff's qualifications and capabilities and their general attitudes and behaviors regarding the turn-around effort would be key factors in determining the quality of SBM's performance. His review of SBM's staff qualifications had been disappointing. In only a few instances did current staff members meet the standards of marketing firms he was familiar with. Most of the current staff had been at the firm for more than a decade, dating back, in fact, to SBM's early history as a very small local marketing concern. The majority had worked for no other company.

The new manager felt that only a handful of the thirty staff members were presently capable of achieving the turn-around desired by the parent company. Two alternative courses of action were immediately apparent. One was to fire everyone and start over. The other was to work directly with the existing staff, to discuss needed changes with them as individuals and as groups, and to try to create a new climate in which to move forward. The manager and his aides decided to follow the second course of action.

The manager's office asked an outside consultant to initiate an OD program for the entire staff, using the Managerial Grid® to help institute an ideal culture fully involving the staff and the new management. The aim of this program was to give the firm a two-year period of rapid but orderly and constructive change. As the first step of this program, a week-long Phase I Managerial Grid laboratory was held at SBM for all the 35 existing staff members.

In the laboratory setting of Phase I the 35 participants undertook a comparative examination of alternative individual behavioral styles. This was done primarily through the use of style questionnaires followed by group activities. During this concentrated, week-long Grid seminar, the instrumented tasks which emphasized group problem-solving behavior were performed by participants with a high degree of candor, members openly exchanging views about task process and individual behavior.

The objective during this period, according to the Grid consultant, was to perfect an organizational climate which would (1) promote and sustain efficient performance of highest quality and quantity, (2) foster and utilize creativity, (3) stimulate enthusiasm for effort, experimentation, innovation, and change, (4) take educational advantage from interaction situations, and (5) look for and find new challenges.

Throughout Phase I severe conflict was evident among participants, both in the smaller groups and when they joined for the general session. Despite the attention in this phase to group problem solving, levels of suspicion, hostility, and defensiveness were extremely high among the staff. The emphasis on candor led the old guard to repeated verbal attacks on the new manager and his aides, who suddenly found themselves in an open and unexpected conflict with the staff. Rather than seeing a new culture emerge from the old, members of the new manager's office found themselves defining a new and different organizational climate which was resisted by those who had known the old climate. Indeed, so great was the gap between the development attempts of the new manager and the behavior patterns of the existing staff that an organized staff group attempted to go over his head to the home office to seek his replacement.

Whether or not individuals gained any behavioral learning or changed behavior from the Phase I Grid experience, it clearly did not develop among the staff a commitment to pursue the developmental program further. Moreover, the manager and his aides were so discomforted by the new candor of the staff and by their resistance that they did not support further pursuit of the Grid program.

It was decided that so immediate and pressing were the business concerns at SBM that investment in a major developmental program at that time would be foolhardy, and the OD effort was abandoned after Phase I.

The failure of the Grid OD program in SBM was perhaps less a fault of the program itself than of SBM and its members. However, we see in this failure some of the difficulties that are encountered when the properties of packaged approaches to OD meet the realities of an organizational change context. At SBM the packaged program was mechanistic and insensitive to the needs and abilities of the participants. The program was a vehicle for raising issues but not resolving them, and it did not adequately develop resolution skills among the participants. While it is often easier to illustrate the working of a particular strategy by reference to a success story, it is just as often more revealing to illustrate them by reference to a failure, as in this case.

One should hasten to note, however, that packaged programs are among the most popular OD approaches in the field today. This popularity is not unfounded, for their successes are well documented. This is particularly true of the Grid Organization Development program. Managers who have employed packaged programs usually report great success, although critics point out that this enthusiasm may be merely a case of a self-fulfilling and self-rewarding prophecy.

Scoring Packaged Approaches to OD

Because packaged programs are so well articulated, it is possible to be quite definitive in assessing their positions on the major criteria important to managers.

Mention has already been made of the highly *structured* a priori plans and procedures of packaged programs. The case illustrated above was not long enough to show the full range of phased activity, but the earlier description of the Blake and Mouton plan clearly indicates the highly controlled character of the packaged approach to OD.

As the SBM case shows, packaged programs start at the top. They wait to be initiated by executives before moving throughout the organization. The case is perhaps a better illustration of the fact that packaged programs may also stop at the top, if management support is necessary for the further movement of the program throughout the organization. The highly controlled nature of packaged programs is conducive to the *unilateral*, from-the-top-down conception and utilization of organizational power, and this is what is found in the practice of packaged approaches to OD.

Rigid plans and controlled, often "instrumented," procedures combine to make packaged approaches to OD relatively *impersonal.* In most instances, involvement in issues of personal relationships would lead the program astray from the plan and is therefore discouraged. The case above is an exception, but an exception which requires note. At times packaged programs, with their low-risk instrumentation, provide a means for individuals to reveal information about personal relationships causing problems for the organization. Once revealed, this information is often difficult to fit into the rigorous plan of a packaged program, which can make it dysfunctional in its effect.

The pace of the packaged program is *incremental.* It starts with the individual, the micro level, and moves on to issues of organization strategy and policy, the macro level. This movement is slow and time consuming and may extend over years. There are only a few organizations which have completed the six phases of the Managerial Grid OD program, though countless others have started Phase I.

In packaged program approaches to OD, the professional relationship between client and consultant is clearly *consultant-centered.* The consultant's picture of the ideal organization provides the goals for the OD effort. The consultant's idea of how this ideal organization can be achieved shapes the activities of organization members in pursuit of OD. The consultant then provides the instruments for these activities, determines when the organization will do what, and controls the progression from one phase to another. And ultimately the consultant is the judge of the organization's success at the completion of a phase. This strong dependence on the consultant of the packaged approach gives OD its closest approximation to the medical model of consultancy.

Like its medical model, a packaged approach to OD comes at a very dear price. It is relatively *expensive* because it invests a considerable amount of organizational time and energy in affairs and activities which may well be extraneous to the real problems of the organization if the effort is not brought to a successful conclusion. In a six- or ten- or twelve-phase program, there may be considerable time and energy invested in the completion of half of those phases, but if the program is stopped at this stage, the consequent payoff will be relatively small in comparison with what might have been received at the conclusion of the full program. Therefore, we must regard packaged programs as relatively *high in price.*

Finally, there are the performance criteria. Because of the wide variation in packaged programs, this evaluation is necessarily somewhat vague. Some programs focus strongly on production-related behaviors; an example of this is the Flexitime Intervention, which deals with flexible working hours and the resultant benefits in terms of productive employee behavior. Management by objectives programs may be said to be more product-oriented than process-oriented in their performance criteria, while a program like the organizational Grid is probably most appropriately judged by process criteria. If one were forced to make a general choice of the performance criteria applicable to most packaged approaches to OD, *process* criteria would probably be most appropriate.

This concludes our examination of packaged approaches to OD. We have focused on the Blake and Mouton Grid Organization Development program as a typical approach, and we have made no attempt to do justice to the full variety of packaged programs currently available. By simply referring to their incoming mail, managers will find a number of programs vying for their attention and their development dollars. Most of them we have not even mentioned here. Their absence should not be read as an indictment of the value of these programs any more so than mention here should be viewed as endorsement. Managers must view each program on its merits for their specific developmental needs and organizational contexts. By applying our seven critical criteria to any packaged programs which chance to cross his desk, any manager can make an objective assessment of the pros and cons in much the same manner as we assessed the Grid Organization Development program.

THE SOCIO-TECHNICAL SYSTEMS APPROACH TO OD

The socio-technical systems (STS) approach to OD is one of the newest alternatives in the field. Up to now it has been practiced by relatively few American firms, but it is quite popular in Europe, where it is associated with the Tavistock group of England. In this country the socio-technical systems group at the University of California, Los Angeles, has been most active. STS is a complex and comprehensive approach to organizational change and development. Relatively little has been written about the application and results of this approach. As more American production firms begin to be involved in STS we can expect more information to appear and consultants' knowledge of the approach and managers' interest in it to increase.

Defining STS

The socio-technical systems approach to OD attempts to achieve the "best fit" between what are believed to be the two interlocking dimensions of any production system—the technical system and its accompanying social system. The basic assumption of the STS approach is that in any production system there are two primary forms of organization; the technological organization, which includes the equipment, materials, and the production process layout; and the work organization, which consists of individuals who staff the technological organizations. Changes in one cannot be pursued independently of changes in the other.

Both the technological organization and the work organization place limits on the efficiency and effectiveness of the firm. These limits must be removed and certain social and psychological forces must be present in the work organization in order to evoke maximum organizational performance from the technological organization.

Three conditions are believed to be necessary in order to maximize organizational performance: (1) workers must have a sense of completion in finishing a meaningful unit of work; (2) workers must hold some control over their own activities; and (3) workers must have satisfactory relationships with others performing related tasks. These properties are assumed to be true of individuals as well as of groups, which can provide a vehicle for the development of these properties in the work organization. Because it holds these conditions to be necessary in order to maximize organizational performance, the STS approach to OD sets about developing technological and sociopsychological conditions encouraging these three features in the organization.

In operational terms, the socio-technical systems approach to OD tries to create an organizational system in which the technical aspects of the work can be arranged in such a manner that the immediate work group experiences (1) completion of a meaningful unit of activity, (2) some degree of responsibility for their task, and (3) satisfactory interpersonal relationships. Specific STS strategies employed to bring about these changes are alterations in work flow patterns, changes in hierarchical relationships, modifications of formal communication systems, redesign of labor and inventory systems, introduction of job enrichment and enlargement, and creation of semiautonomous work groups.

Many managers are familiar with this last strategy because of the publicity given semiautonomous work groups in Swedish automobile production plants. Semiautonomous work groups are also employed extensively in Yugoslav factories and by a major dog food and soap producer here in the United States. It is important to emphasize that extensive reports of large-scale STS OD programs in American firms have yet to be released. We can anticipate learning much from the results of these major programs. There are already, however, many instances of STS principles being applied in organizations on a smaller scale, which can also be instructive. One such instance is described in the following case.

A Socio-Technical Systems OD Case

Peoples Plumbing is the fictitious name of a West Coast manufacturer of do-it-yourself plumbing kits sold in convenience hardware stores throughout the western United States. The products of Peoples Plumbing fall into four categories: toilet, sink, faucet, and outdoor sprinkler. At the opening of our story the company was operating in the manner described below.

At the small production facility workers assembling kits in each of these four areas drew on a common parts bay, where the requisite pipe joints, washers, and such were manufactured and warehoused. Each product line uses basically the same parts, although some are cut to different dimensions and specifications. It was the responsibility of the manufacturing center to plan its activities so that no product line ran short of the requisite parts for kit assembly. Such shortages could cause slowdowns and in some instances force a line to shut down. From even this simplified description it is obvious that workers in the individual product lines were completely dependent upon the manufacturing center. Consequently the speed of their output, its amount, and even its quality are functions of the speed, amount, and quality of parts produced in the manufacturing center.

Of the four product lines, sprinkler kits had the greatest demand and the highest profit margin, followed by the faucet, sink, and toilet kits, in that order. Production priorities in the manufacturing center followed the same order. As a result of the manufacturing center's priority on providing necessary parts for the faucet and outdoor sprinkler groups, the sink and toilet production groups frequently ran out of the parts they needed. This led to a great deal of intergroup competition. In some instances production materials were stolen and there were even suspected cases of sabotage of rival product lines. Morale among workers in the low-priority product lines was very low and turnover among all employees was quite high.

Management, in assessing the problem, decided that one alternative was to buy additional production equipment, and a consultant was hired to do a feasibility study of such a capital investment. After closer diagnosis of the situation, the consultant, an STS specialist, felt that the evident social problems were as important as the technological problems presented by the production process. In an attempt to give workers a sense of completion in finishing a meaningful unit of work, some control over their own activities, and satisfactory relationships with those performing other tasks, the consultant and the firm decided to experiment with semiautonomous work groups.

Each production group met to decide which parts they felt were absolutely essential to have under the control of their group, parts critical to their production effectiveness. In each case this amounted to no more than four or five of the component parts of a kit, with a kit's total number of parts sometimes running as high as 18. The bulk of the component parts—washers, screws, and the like—remained interchangeable between kits for faucets, sinks, toilets, and outdoor sprinklers.

Production equipment for these essential parts was moved to where the dependent kits were assembled, and control over production of these parts was given to the assembly workers, who were then responsible for the flow of parts into the assembly area. Where necessary, assembly workers were also trained in the operation of the equipment. In addition, each work unit was told that profits realized from increased productivity would be applied by each group to the purchase of equipment necessary for the production of all the component parts needed by that group. For example, through increased production, in time the sink kit assembly group might come to have control of all the production facilities required for all parts in its kits. As soon as one group gained control of its own parts production, the demand for parts on the main manufacturing group would slacken and the other groups would increase their production, which would enable them to gain control of their own production facilities.

This experiment has been under way for a year. Until now, only one assembly unit has been able to increase its productivity sufficiently to purchase and have control over all the machinery required to produce the component parts in the kit. Interestingly enough, this group is the toilet kit assembly, traditionally a low-profit, low-demand item for Peoples Plumbing. In this product group the experiment has had the desired effect. Because of the removal of the demands of the toilet kit group, the central manufacturing group has been able to provide the remaining three assembly units with a continuous flow of the requisite parts. Significant increases in the productivity of these groups have been made, and they too are moving rapidly toward total control of parts production for their products.

It is important to emphasize that throughout this process the consultant worked very closely with the workers in the production center and on the assembly line in order to learn which tasks and processes they felt to be most important. This spirit of worker contribution to the design of the experiment continued through its implementation. Morale is up throughout the organization, turnover is down, and employees report a new sense of meaning in their work, a new feeling of control over what they do, and improved relationships with their coworkers. Management is understandably very pleased with the improved productivity.

This brief example of STS OD in a small production plant may present this approach as simpler and less comprehensive than it originally seemed. Indeed, one of the beauties of STS is that it can be implemented in small organizations with relative ease. The problems of implementing such a combined technological and sociological approach obviously multiply as the size and complexity of the organization increase. However, whether STS is applied in a small or large organization, in a production or a service organization, the basic characteristics remain the same and are well illustrated by the case of Peoples Plumbing.

Scoring the Socio-Technical Systems Approach to OD

As the consultant's procedure at Peoples Plumbing indicated, the STS approach to OD begins with a specific orientation toward what is wrong with the organization and what needs to be done. This is manifested in a rather *structured plan* for diagnosing the problem and intervening in the organization to bring about the conditions of an ideal socio-technical system. Alteration in the technological process of the organization alone implies a degree of planning and specificity that is not found in other approaches to OD. When one adds to the technological system an interface with the organization's social system, the demand for detailed planning increases. This detail is a fundamental feature of the socio-technical systems approach.

A second fundamental feature of the STS approach is its striving for conditions under which workers share in the responsibility for their work. Clearly, *power* in the STS OD effort is *shared*. Managers who consider STS must recognize that in so doing they implicitly agree to share with their workers power over the production processes of the organization. Many managers and workers alike find such arrangements uncomfortable.

In theory, STS promotes the importance of satisfactory interpersonal relationships in the work situation. In practice, however, the approach generally focuses on the structural and technical dimensions of the organization and of worker interrelationships. The nature of personal relationships in the STS approach might best be characterized as *impersonal to personal work,* with more emphasis on personal. Personal relationships outside the domain of task relationships are not considered in the STS approach to OD.

The pace of STS OD is very much dependent on the size of the organization. In Peoples Plumbing, changes took place rapidly because the organization was small and there was ample opportunity for the consultant's hands-on contact with the organization. As the size of the organization increases, this opportunity diminishes. Much more work must be invested in creating worker readiness and exploring alternative designs. Generating worker participation in the process also takes considerable time, for more workers must be involved. We must therefore say that the pace of STS is predominately an *incremental* one.

The price of STS in terms of its opportunity costs can be quite high. Considerable time must be spent in providing everyone in the organization, from production workers to the very top managers, ample opportunity to participate in the redesign of the technological and sociological systems. This is expensive time, time which might better, in the eyes of some managers, be spent in the day-to-day management and production activities. Other managers would find this time a small investment for the kind of payoff possible to be gained through STS. Whatever the case, both groups would agree that STS is an *expensive* approach to OD.

In STS, responsibility for direction of the program is *dual,* shared between client and consultant. In a typical case, the consultant brings to the client considerable expertise in the design of social systems, but he must rely on the client to provide the technological expertise necessary for the redesign effort. By pooling their technological and sociological expertise, the consultant and the client can arrive at the ideal conditions STS seeks.

It is clear that STS, more than the other approaches to OD, attempts to contribute directly to production efficiency and effectiveness. At the same time, STS claims a major contribution to the organization's effective processes. Therefore, the performance of an STS OD program can appropriately be measured on both *product and process* dimensions. Because the socio-technical systems approach to OD is the newest of the alternative approaches, these characteristics may change in time as experimentation with the STS method continues. For now, in the few cases we are aware of, these appear to be the predominant features of the STS approach to OD.

THE TRANSACTIONAL ANALYSIS APPROACH TO OD

Spurred by the success of transactional analysis (TA) in customer relations and supervisory training programs, many managers have looked to TA for organization development. This application is a relatively recent development for both TA and OD, and as yet it has been implemented in only a few organizations. As the popularity of TA training programs increases—and all current signs point in this direction—attempts to use the TA approach in OD will similarly increase in frequency.

It is neither possible nor intended to present transactional analysis theory in detail here. The manager who has not been exposed to TA may want to refer to some of the standard literature of the field if he wants to give serious consideration to TA OD. Managers with a fundamental grasp of TA and its language will have no difficulty understanding the TA approach to OD and assessing its appropriateness for their organizations.

TA OD Defined

One of the fundamental bases of TA is the concept of "scripts." An individual's script is his preconscious life-plan, unconsciously selected in early childhood, which governs the general course of his life in much the same way as a theatrical script governs the action of a play. It is assumed that in the life of every individual the dramatic life events, the roles that are learned, rehearsed, and acted out, are determined by the individual's script. Scripts are selected, which means that individuals are free to alter scripts or select new ones, if they choose to do so. In TA, script changes *must* precede behavior changes.

In applying TA to OD, consultants have expanded on the idea of individual scripts to postulate the existence of *organizational scripts* which likewise govern the events and behavior of the organization and which likewise must be changed if the organization is to change. Determination of the organization's script is used to find where organizational change is necessary and desired. It is another way of finding answers to the OD questions: Where are we? Where do we want to be?

Thomas Clary is one of the foremost practitioners of TA OD. He asks the following kinds of questions to determine an organization's script, giving them a dramatized framework:[6]

> *Prologue.* (To get the participants in the mood to think about their organization.)
> 1. What original philosophies and policies in the organization have now become traditional and sacred?

[6] Thomas C. Clary, "Script Analysis: A New Approach to OD," in Dorothy Jongeward, Ed., *Everybody Wins: TA Applied to Organizations* (Reading, Mass.: Addison-Wesley, 1973).

2. Who was responsible for setting them?
3. For what purpose were they established?
   (a) What were they expected to accomplish?
   (b) What was the purpose given?
   (c) What do you think was their *real* purpose?

Act I. Setting the Stage. (Identifying the physical setting, the characters, their roles and costumes, the premise for their actions, and their internal and external conflicts as they affect the organization or as the organization affects them.)
1. What is the setting?
2. Name and describe each major character involved.

Act II. The Action. (Setting into motion the conflicts, avoidances, and other problems that may exist.)
1. Show how each conflict, isolation, or other problem comes about, based on the information discovered in Act I.
2. Explain how each character is trying to work through these problems.

Act III. The Resolution. (In Clary's view, this act discloses how the organizational script can be changed if there is a desire and a commitment to change it.)

Participants move into a problem-solving mode focused on an evolving commitment to change parts of the organizational script which have been found to contain problems, and through this to create a new and healthier organizational script. The brief case reported below shows how script analysis as an approach to OD can illuminate major organizational problems and point out the direction for positive change.

A TA OD Case

R's is a major department store in a Midwest metropolitan area. It has long been the least successful store in town, despite good locations, quality merchandise, and competitive prices. The poor profit performance at R's has been attributed to the very stiff department store competition in the area. In an attempt to bolster sales, the management of R's contracted for TA training of sales personnel. An extended training program was initiated, but it soon became evident that even successful training of sales personnel would have impact on only a small portion of the organization's profit problem. There appeared to be major problems in salesperson-supervisor-management relations, in store-headquarters interaction, and in organizational structure. In short, there emerged a clear need for a total effort toward organizational improvement.

The consultants decided to continue with the TA approach, building on employees' recent experience with TA training. Groups established at the management, supervisor, and salesperson level began to determine the organization's script. In each group, members addressed questions patterned after Clary, first individually, then in open group discussion. The resultant script data were surprising in the breadth and depth to which it was felt by members that R's was playing out a "loser's" script.

R's was viewed by employees as the least desirable of the department stores in town, "the ugly stepsister," "the orphan," "the beggar." Many saw R's as an employer of last resort because they had not been hired by competitors. As one manager put it, "I tried to get in a Broadway play, but the best I could do was Newark!" This losing self-image was projected to customers. "They only shop us because the other stores are sold out of whatever they're looking for." R's was not only an employer of last resort, but a shopping stop of last resort as well. Organization members found nothing but support for the losing script in corporate reports, which showed ample evidence of R's poor performance.

Confronted with clear evidence of such overwhelming negativism, management immediately began to build organizational self-esteem on all fronts. This effort started with a commitment in the OD effort to pursue a "winning" — "we try harder" — script in which the ugly stepsister turns into a ravishing beauty sought by all the suitors in the land. This script change was immediately supported by a wide variety of actions:

"Exclusive" representation of several prestige lines was secured.
Recruiting and hiring coups over the competition were publicized.
Outstanding employee performances were recognized.
Challenging but realistic "turnaround goals" were established.
A store-wide clean-up, spruce-up campaign was carried out.

As of today the new script seems to have taken hold; morale and profits are up. The real test will come in the organization's reaction to whatever setbacks may be brought on by circumstances beyond the control of organization members. For the short term, TA OD has been effective for R's department store.

Scoring TA OD

TA is a well-articulated, highly structured system for analyzing and altering human behavior. The same degree of structure is true of TA in an organizational context. Diagnosing organizational scripts follows a *detailed plan* often specifying a specific structure for questions and discussion.

Power in TA OD is assumed to be *shared.* Organizational scripts are not selected unilaterally but by the total organizational membership, albeit implicitly. If the script is to be changed, the change must similarly be supported by the total organizational membership even though the impetus for change may come from the top.

The orientation of TA OD is toward macro organizational phenomena. Personal relationships are the focus of TA training but tend to be set aside when TA turns to organizational scripts. TA OD is most often *impersonal.*

Organization members may decide on a new script literally overnight, but developing and displaying supportive new behaviors takes much longer. The pace of TA OD is, therefore, *incremental.*

Visualizing organizational action as the enactment of a script falls considerably outside the day-to-day activities of most organizations. Time spent doing this may have high payoffs, but where it does not the diversion, although entertaining, can be very costly. The price of TA OD is *moderate to expensive.*

The consultant in TA OD initiates the questioning, but leaves it to the members of the organization to extend the metaphor and assess its validity. Inasmuch as an organizational script is the property of the organization's members, the professional relationship between the client and the consultant in TA OD is dominated by the client.

If one accepts the idea that the script dominates organizational life, then one should expect changes in the script to be reflected in all facets of the organization. The criteria for assessing the performance of TA OD must be both *product and process,* although in practice effects on processes appear to be more frequent than ones on products.

SUMMING UP

The completed chart in Figure 24 summarizes the descriptions of the seven currently popular approaches to OD. Some qualifying comments are in order.

First, the chart *describes* the available alternative approaches to OD; it *does not evaluate* them. Evaluation is the responsibility of the manager weighing the characteristics of the various approaches against organizational needs and resources. Each of these approaches is supported by sound theoretical underpinnings, each has registered both successes and failures in organizations of every description, and each is currently being used in organizations. These present efforts will contribute to the continuing evolution of the approaches. No one approach is better than the others for all organizations. There is only a "best" approach for a specific organization at a specific time.

Figure 24. Summary of OD approaches.

Alternative Approaches to OD	Nature of the Plan Structured Sequentially structured Unstructured	Nature of Power Unilateral Shared Delegated	Nature of Personal Relationships Impersonal Personal-Work Personal
Survey Feedback	Structured	Unilateral	Impersonal
Process Consultation	Unstructured	Shared	Personal-Work
Team Building	Sequentially structured	Unilateral	Work
Laboratory Training	Unstructured	Shared	Personal
Packaged approaches	Structured	Unilateral	Impersonal
Socio-Technical Systems	Structured	Shared	Impersonal to Personal-Work
Transactional Analysis	Structured	Shared	Impersonal

Second, the *general* and *relative* character of the assessments of individual approaches must be considered. Different consultants will use process consultation in different ways, and one specific PC OD effort may have little in common with another; in *general,* however, process consultation appears as we have described it here. Similarly, for a given OD approach the assessments here are made *relative* to other OD approaches; it would be very difficult to determine with any degree of precision to what extent team building is sequentially structured, yet in relation to the unstructured character of laboratory training and the structured character of packaged programs, description of TB as "sequentially structured" is clearly appropriate. Because they are general and relative, it should be emphasized that these assessments are *guidelines,* not sets of fixed rules.

Finally, as in any survey review, some approaches that have been excluded perhaps should not have been (MBO and Flexitime, possibly) and others that are included perhaps need not have been (laboratory training). Our intention is not to review *all* the possible approaches to OD, which would be neither possible nor particularly useful; it is to review the most popular approaches, the ones most likely to come to the attention of managers today, and to provide a framework within which managers can assess and evaluate other approaches to OD as the need arises.

These qualifications noted, how can managers use this "consumer's guide" to OD? How can it help them answer the important questions our presentation

Nature of Pace	Nature of Price	Nature of Professional Relationships	Nature of Performance Criteria
Evolutionary	Inexpensive	Client centered	Product
Incremental	Moderate	Dual	Product-Process
Rapid	Expensive	Consultant centered	Process
Incremental	Moderate	1. Consultant 2. Client	Process
Evolutionary	Inexpensive	Consultant	Process
Incremental	Moderate	1. Consultant 2. Client	1. Process 2. Product
Evolutionary	Expensive	Client	Process
Incremental	Expensive	Consultant	Process
Incremental	Expensive	1. Consultant 2. Client	1. Product 2. Process
Incremental	Moderate to expensive	Client	1. Product 2. Process

has raised repeatedly: First, how do I choose an OD approach? How do I discover which OD approach is best for my organization? and second, Once I've chosen an approach, how do I implement it and integrate it into organizational activities? How do I manage OD?

The next two chapters answer these questions.

CHAPTER 6

Some Criteria of Effective Approaches to OD: Making the Choice

How is a manager to choose among these many approaches to OD? How is he to decide which of these competing and complementing change strategies is most appropriate for his organization? As one manager commented after reviewing the many alternatives, "I know that no one of these approaches is best for *all* organizations *all* the time, but just tell me which one is best for *my* organization at *this* time." There is no quick and easy response to his demand.

The "best approach to OD in a given organization at a given time is dependent on many variables, which may be broadly grouped into two classes of choice criteria. One class includes criteria that relate to the "fit" between the OD approach and the organization. Here the manager must consider the procedures of the various alternative approaches, as described in Chapter 5, and whether his organization and his people are ready and able to work with and profit from these procedures. For example, organizations with stable markets and production processes may be more comfortable with a structured, preplanned approach to OD. Similarly, more turbulent organizational environments may call for quite flexible change plans. The fit sought here is between the characteristics of the organization and the characteristics of the OD approach. These qualities constitute one set of choice criteria.

The choice criteria of the second class, the subject of this chapter, are more general in character. They deal with the prerequisites of effective change in today's organizations and could be called "contemporary contextual criteria of effective organization." They are the factors with which effective OD approaches and strategies must cope. They are also, obviously, the factors managers must consider in picking an OD approach.

The problem at the heart of the search for an effective approach to OD is that the criteria of effective intervention in one organizational context at one time may not be valid in another (or even the same) organizational context at another time. We want to explore here some key change criteria suggested by the conditions prevalent in postindustrial organizations.

The search for criteria of effective interventions is neither recent in origin nor random in direction. In the field today the criteria most generally accepted by managers and consultants alike seem to be those suggested by Chris Argyris: To be effective, OD must generate valid information, ensure free informed choice, and promote internal commitment.

Argyris contends, and many others in the field concur, that these are essential processes and must be fulfilled if any organizational change is to be effective, regardless of the organization or substantive issues involved. These criteria are central to effective intervention. As managers are quick to see, however, these criteria are inherently contextual in character and are of only minimal aid in selecting the intervention strategies most appropriate to a given organizational problem.

The task as managers see it is to take Argyris' criteria a step further, to explore the requirements of valid information, free informed choice, and internal commitment within the framework of what we know about contemporary organizations and their members. Implied in the definition of this task is the idea that the way these criteria are currently viewed is inconsistent with the conditions faced by managers in most modern organizations. This point deserves elaboration.

As we discussed in Chapter 2, OD emerged and matured over the course of what are now viewed as the final 15 years of the industrial era in the United States. Many currently popular views of organizational change are products of this era and reflect the "reformist" model, which was the predominant concept of organizational change in the industrial era. In the reformist model organizational problems, like social and political problems, are basically questions of "how to put right what is wrong." Answers are viewed as either known or knowable, and change is a process of managers learning and implementing correct solutions. This reformist orientation is evident in OD approaches which rely greatly upon direction and control by external "experts" to correct organizational functioning. Such a view assumes the following contextual conditions to be true for Argyris' effective change criteria: (1) The generation of valid information is the function and property of the expert consultant, not of the manager and his people; the consultant knows what is right. (2) Free informed choice is ensured by finding out what is right to do and doing it. (Why would a manager and his people choose to do anything but what is right?) (3) Internal commitment will develop as a natural consequence of doing what is right. As these assumptions show, in reformist approaches to OD the primary contextual criteria of effective intervention are concerned with correctness—find out what is "right" and do it!

During the industrial era, and especially during its last 15 years, reformist approaches to organizational change were moderately successful if given the time and resources necessary to make them work. However, the utility of reformist approaches and the value of reformist criteria for effective organizational change are seriously questionable for the conditions most managers face today. These conditions are generally discussed as those of postindustrial society and postindustrial organizations.

The dynamics of postindustrial society most familiar to managers are ever accelerating rates of technological change—the information explosion—and widespread social change—the participation revolution. These act together to increase the number of problems managers must solve and to decrease the time available to solve them. Today's managers are faced simultaneously with the short periods of time in which problems spring up and turn critical, and with decreased human and material resources for solving these problems. They will readily attest to the fact that postindustrial organizational context is far more complex and uncertain than its industrial predecessor. Managers find it more and more difficult to know what information is needed and then more and more difficult to gather it, which makes both operations take much more time. Yet it is precisely now, when more and more organization members demand to participate in organizational action, that the time allowable for these operations is decreasing.

Clearly, the contextual conditions facing the contemporary manager render the reformist orientation to organizational change generally inappropriate and often invalid. Organizations no longer have sufficient time or resources to afford the luxury of reformist approaches. Moreover, the basic problem confronting managers today is less the reformist issue of how to put right what is wrong than it is how to institutionalize change processes. It must be recognized that in postindustrial organizations things once "put right" are very unlikely to stay "right." *Correctability* criteria have therefore become as important for effective intervention as *correctness* criteria, in consonance with the conditions in today's organizational contexts.

In order for an organizational change to generate valid information in today's contexts, it must be action based, be cyclically constructed, and be capable of joining knowledge and action roles. If change strategies are to ensure free informed choice, they must be capable of learning from experience—others as well as their own—but not be bound by it. Finally, the development of internal commitment in today's organizations depends upon providing participative roles in which the consequences of intervention correspond to the risks undertaken. These conditions speak more of how change is managed than of what the change is. For this reason managers need a particularly clear understanding of these OD management criteria if their organizational change and development efforts are to be successful.

In order to intervene effectively in organizational processes, the need for quantities of high-quality information is imperative. Simultaneously, in the ever-changing environment of the modern organization, the time and resources required to procure such data are often prohibitive. Reformist approaches to OD offer two alternatives to the manager faced with this data dilemma. He may act on the basis of inadequate data, risking failure, or he may wait until sufficient data have been gathered, at which point either the problem has become so severe it is immune to change, or the data are no longer relevant because the environment has changed.

Today's organizations require the collection of valid information through action-based approaches. They respond to the data dilemma by continuously taking action on the accepted basis of inadequate data in the knowledge that such action will yield data useful for continuous evolution toward progressively more preferable outcomes.

The variability of data in contemporary organizations thus requires that effective solutions be sought through consecutive and continual managerial action rather than through contemplative design. And it follows that if managerial action toward change is to elicit valid information for the development of consecutively more effective actions, each step must be viewed not only as responding to data but also as generating data. In this perspective, diagnosis and intervention meld; collecting data and acting on data are joined in a managed cycle intended to be self-generating, self-directing, self-monitoring, and self-correcting.

A third condition for gathering valid information in today's organizations emerges from action-based OD approaches cyclically constructed to join data collection and action — that is, these approaches are designed to merge the roles of data collector and actor. When data collection and action are viewed as inherently inseparable, if different people collect data and take action, or if the same people collect data and act but at different times, diagnosis is likely to be impractical and intervention uninformed. This has significant implications for the relationships between the manager, organization members, and the consultant, and it calls for far more collaboration than one finds in most organizational activities.

If change efforts are to ensure free informed choice, they must be designed to allow the manager to learn from experience without being bound by it. Intervention approaches must not constrain his awareness only to those alternatives which have been found to be correct in the past, whether for that organization or for others. Such a limitation not only misinforms the manager, by implying that only past successes have promise for the present, but actually imposes a choice upon him. Effective change strategies must instead encourage and help the manager to develop his own choice criteria, to determine the level of risk appropriate for his own efforts, and to assess his own commitment. With these guidelines he can then evaluate his own experience and the experiences of others. Free informed choice is ensured where the management of the OD process promotes the discarding of experience which is not useful.

It is imperative that OD, which seeks to promote internal commitment to change in contemporary organizations, include, in key roles, parties who by virtue of their organizational position have a right to order action and those who have an obligation to respond to such an order. Members of the modern workforce increasingly view their participation in decisions affecting their organizational lives as a legitimate right of employment. There is also considerable empirical evidence to suggest that this participation is necessary to ensure the degree of commitment required to implement effective interventions. However, merely providing for participative roles is often inadequate. The modern employee is sensitive to co-optation in name only. The consequence of this is more often a decrease rather than an increase in his commitment. It is essential for managers to structure the OD effort so that those who are most likely to bear the risks, benefits, and other consequences participate in the change activity in roles which correspond to the amount of risk they take. Only this can ensure the meaningful participation required for the development of effective internal commitment.

Given what we know about organizations and their members today and what managers experience today, the preceding interpretation of the contextual criteria for effective OD seems appropriate. This interpretation also suggests much regarding the manager's role in the change effort.

Certain dynamics prevalent in all modern organizations must be dealt with if the change effort is to succeed. The responsibility for managing these dynamics and the change effort for the benefit of the organization falls squarely on the shoulders of the manager. Effective organizational change is as much a function of how change is managed as it is of what change is introduced. Once he understands the alternative approaches to OD and selects the one appropriate for his situation, the manager needs to manage the OD effort effectively. Chapter 7 gives managers a model for managing OD which goes far toward ensuring effective introduction, implementation, and integration of OD into their organizations.

CHAPTER 7

Managing Organization Development: A Model for Managers

The flow of any managerial action is continuous from its inception in idea form until it is rejected, succeeds, or fails. This does not mean that managers act on a single problem continuously until it is solved. It only suggests that any organizational act has a history which can be thought of in terms of a time line and the specific sequence of events of which it is composed. A descriptive model of managerial action stops the flow of action to explain its distinct key phases. The phases in model descriptions are merely convenient markers, not rigid divisions, for, as managers know, organizational processes are continuous. Any model of organizational action, including this one of managing OD, lists a sequence of steps, but it does so recognizing that the processes described do not necessarily appear at logically distinct times. Given the fluidity of organizational action, these elements are so interwoven that they may appear together in different ways at different times in the flow.

It is important to keep in mind these general points about descriptive models and their relationship to the managerial processes they depict. Presenting OD management as a model makes it easier to explain the relatively distinct elements of the process and their approximate relationships to each other over time, but it cannot allow for adequate expression of the fluidity and complexity of interrelationships in this or any managerial process. Managers will have to draw on their own experiences to add these dimensions to the model.

There are nine major phases in effectively managing an OD effort in an ongoing organization. They constitute the foundation of the model for managing an approach to OD. Phases 1, 2, and 3 set the "context" for managing the OD effort, while phases 4 through 8 make up the manager's "action step cycle." Phase 9 begins a new action step cycle repeating phases 4 through 8.[1]

---

[1]Michael E. McGill, *Action Research Designs for Development* (Washington, D.C.: NTDS Press, 1973).

Phase 1. Convergence of interest
Phase 2. Establishing the charter
Phase 3. Legitimation and sponsorship
Phase 4. Problem identification
Phase 5. The general plan
Phase 6. Action hypothesis
Phase 7. Action step
Phase 8. Formative evaluation
Phase 9. Problem reidentification.

PHASE 1. CONVERGENCE OF INTEREST

In order for an OD effort to begin in an organization, there must be individuals who have personal (perhaps selfish) motives for examining organizational processes and taking action, ones who are convinced that such an effort will achieve different goals, and others who are of the opinion that the organization should be concerned with its own functioning. These people must be brought together, usually by the initiative of the manager, to share their mutual interests.

The important element here is the convergence of interest around the commitment to gather information and take action, regardless of the individual motives behind this interest. Individuals' initial commitment to organizational research and action is motivated by problems, issues, and/or feelings which are usually of immediate concern only to themselves. What they all have in common is not concern about a specific problem or issue but the desire for information and action in an area that relates to all their separate problems. The manager's first responsibility in an OD effort is to find these organization members and to bring them together. While it is true that such a convergence of interest is to some extent prerequisite for the effectiveness of any managerial effort, it is of special importance in managing OD.

In both theory and operation, the success of any OD effort depends in large part upon the participants' commitment to act on data about the organization. The earlier this commitment emerges and the stronger it is, the greater are the chances that the approach to OD will be effective. Also, the initial convergence of interest sets the pattern for the management steps which follow. In other management activities, convergence of interest may represent little more than a license to begin the process. But in managing OD, convergence is a critical initial phase which provides an indicator of probable success and establishes a pattern for the management activities that follow.

The importance of convergence of interest in an OD effort is further emphasized when one considers its implications in developing a relationship with an outside consultant. A consultant becomes involved with an organization in one of two ways. Either he makes the organization aware of its need for his services and procures an invitation to enter, or the organization, on its own, becomes aware of its need for outside assistance and invites him to enter. In the former case, the consultant often "creates" a convergence of interest, usually by drawing the attention of top-level organization officials to their need for information and action on certain issues. Here the initiative for OD lies with the consultant. In the latter entry pattern, convergence of interest is often at organizational levels far removed from the top, and it appears before the consultant is present on the scene. Individuals seeking information and action on their own problems join with others who need similar research and action. This is usually done on a very informal basis under the auspices of the manager. As this group feels their needs for information or action expanding beyond the scope of their skill or expertise, they look for outside assistance. The initiative in establishing a relationship with a consultant lies with the manager and members of the organization.

The latter pattern of entry is both characteristic of and critical to effective OD. Participants' responsibility for initiating the OD effort sets the pattern for and strengthens their ultimate responsibility for executing the program and ensuring its effectiveness. The consultant who engineers an invitation may in the process engineer an artificial commitment that will adversely affect the ultimate OD program, at significant cost to the manager and his organization. The pitfalls of false commitment are not as common where consultant entry follows rather than precedes convergence of interest.

It is usually on the entry of the outside consultant following the convergence of interest that the OD effort begins to be formalized and leads to phase 2 of the process.

PHASE 2. ESTABLISHING THE CHARTER

Through their convergence of interest the manager forms a group which is concerned with initiating data and action processes leading toward organizational improvement. We shall call this group the organization development team. Its creation leads to the development of a common frame of reference within which the OD process flows. This frame requires (1) a basis for internal organization—that is, membership in the OD team—(2) establishment of common group ends or goals, and (3) definition of the contractual relationship with the consultant. These constitute the "charter" of the OD team.

Ideally, the OD team would include all those in the focal group who have either the right to initiate managerial action or the obligation to respond. As a matter of practical management, this is seldom possible. Initial composition of the OD team is determined by the convergence of interest among organization members. The OD team should be a voluntary group, though the manager may particularly want to encourage key people to participate. Despite encouragement, many in the organization may not want to take part. The problem here for the manager is to ensure that their input is represented in the OD team even though they do not participate directly.

It would be rare (though not unheard-of) for every member of a group or organization to be sufficiently motivated to participate in an OD team. When this happens, the manager is faced with a problem of a different sort. A group of unwieldy size would thwart the effectiveness of an OD team by hampering interaction and discussion. One answer to the problem of size may be the division of responsibility among several OD teams, with a representative central steering group headed by the manager. For example, where the OD effort is organization-wide and the desire to participate widespread, OD teams could be formed within natural work units, with representatives from these groups sitting on an OD steering team responsible for overall coordination.

Whether the membership issue be one of too few or too many in the OD team, a sensible and feasible guideline is that each OD team must include representatives of all groups. All members of the OD team should be equal regardless of their organizational positions or functions.

If the OD team is to pursue effectively its interest in information and action on organizational issues, it must define team goals. These are distinct from the aspirations and motives of individual OD team members, even though they naturally play a part in setting group goals. This first and very important OD team step, formulating group goals, starts exploring, discussing, and modifying an idea until it finally becomes a group goal. Here we will consider elements of the goal-setting process which have particular importance in managing an OD effort and in the work of the OD team. Under the manager's guidance, the OD team should keep the following questions in mind as it formulates goals for the OD effort.

1. Does the statement of the goal include:
   (a) The object or target of group action?
   (b) The source of the goal—who has set or determined it?
   (c) The kind of participation required of organization members?
   (d) The outcome sought?
2. Have all group members had some part in the selection of the goal?
3. Do all members see the goal in the same way?
4. Are the goals consistent with the parent organization's goals?
5. Are the goals reasonable? Can the team expect to approach them within the given time and resources?

6. Is there provision for orienting new members to the goals?
7. Is there provision to modify or change the goals as a result of experience?

These questions refer to the process of setting goals as much as to the content of those goals. In practice goal setting is more flexible and largely a natural outgrowth of the particular membership and context of the OD teams. However, the criteria for establishing the kinds of goals to be set have been substantiated in OD work and deserve amplification.

It is important to emphasize that OD goals are distinct from specific problems. Goals refer to the overall direction or general concern which gives a common framework for subsequent activities. They provide a helpful orientation for the OD effort, effectively focusing and coordinating the other phases, including problem identification. Goals facilitate management of the OD effort. This much understood, two additional criteria that are only implied above should be emphasized.

First, the goals settled on by the OD team must be both important to the group and significant for the total organization. Settlement on concerns of little importance may come easily to the diversely motivated OD team members, but it is unlikely to foster the degree of commitment required for an effective OD program. Acceptance of meaningful goals will doubtless be harder but will also contribute to commitment to pursue the goals. This commitment is critical to effective OD and stems, in large part, from the nature of the goals and the attitude that they evoke in organization members, who must feel that "doing this will be worthwhile."

In addition to evoking the belief that they are worthwhile, the goals should also be regarded as "feasible" or "reasonable" or "manageable." The meaning is in all cases the same: given the limitations on the OD team, including (but not confined to) available time and resources, these goals can be achieved. Unrealistic, unreachable goals evoke little commitment; few individuals will involve themselves in efforts predestined to fall short of their purpose and fewer managers would lead such efforts. Where there is a feeling that goals *can* be achieved, and where both the availability and the accessibility of appropriate means can be seen, there is concomitant commitment to see that they *are* achieved.

Another criterion for OD goals is acceptable justification of the need and right to pursue the goals as stated. While individual members of the OD team will have numerous reasons for their involvement, these are not necessarily acceptable justifications for the team as a whole to use in establishing its collective right to pursue its goals. In order to obtain full acceptance of the goals and commitment to their achievement, the goals must be justifiable.

This takes on additional importance when the OD team asks the organization at large for sponsorship. Justification may come before or after agreement on goals, as a single logical postulate or as a series of rationalizations, but in any case it is essential to the viability of the goals selected by the OD team.

Deciding team membership and setting goals are two core activities which do much to shape subsequent actions. The third step during this phase also influences the course of the overall effort. To finish establishing the charter, the contract between client and consultant must be negotiated.

Contractual negotiations between client and consultant deal with two basic considerations, the formal contract and the psychological contract. The formal contract settles how much time will be devoted to consultation and over how long a period, what general services will be performed, and what form and amount of payment will be made. These are largely matters of client circumstances and consultant discretion. They will vary widely from case to case and need not concern us here. Any observation we might make would have only limited general applicability. The "psychological contract," however, deserves considerable attention from managers because it deals with critical expectations—what the client expects from the relationship and what the consultant expects.

First, there is the question of who is the client in OD. In most OD programs the client is the individual or group who asks the consultant in and to whom the consultant reports. Usually this person or group is near or at the top of the organizational hierarchy. Often it is the OD team that initially contacts the consultant and works immediately with him. The OD team, composed as it is either of all those who are organizationally empowered to initiate action or obligated to respond or of representatives of these groups, is (or should be) truly representative of the larger client system. Thus the true client is the total organization even though the immediate working relationship is between the consultant and the OD team. This point is important because it influences the availability of the work of the OD team in addition to affecting the commitment and involvement of those not immediately participating in the process. One OD consultant uses the rule that *all* data gathered is presented and made available to *all* people in the system, and he does this as much to increase the visibility of the OD effort, in the hope of generating a "multiplier effect" throughout the organization, as to acknowledge that the total organization is the client.

What can the organization, as client, expect from the consultant in an OD effort? The client may reasonably expect

Commitment to working toward organizational improvement.
Skills and expertise which will be available to the client when needed.

Values, attitudes, and beliefs which cannot be separated from the application of skills and expertise.

Restraint not to make promises or encourage expectations he cannot reasonably expect to fulfill.

Respect, throughout the process, for the client's right to self-determination.

Efforts to develop in the client and the client system skills which enable the client to pursue a program of organizational improvement after the departure of the consultant.

The consultant in an OD effort also has certain expectations of the client. Among these are:

Commitment to organizational improvement and a concomitant willingness to explore alternative attitudes and behaviors.

Willingness to diagnose and examine problems openly and honestly.

Willingness to recognize the consultant's skills and values, and having done so to allow him a role of equal influence (not greater or lesser than that of organization members) in organizational decisions in the context of the OD effort.

Willingness to acquire the skills and knowledge which would enable the client to pursue organizational improvement as a regular, continuing organizational function without the aid of a consultant.

In these lists of respective client and consultant expectations, those which deal with the skills and values of the consultant and the manner in which these are exercised in the OD program depart most radically from the norms of contracts managers usually negotiate with consultants. They therefore deserve additional explanation. At issue in these parts is recognition, by client and consultant alike, that OD is, by definition and operation, a normative, value-laden process. Rather than attempt an artificial separation between the skills and values of the consultant, effective management of OD attempts to provide for their meaningful input as a means and expression of free and conscious choice. To the extent that the values of the consultant are imposed upon the client, free choice is restricted. To the extent that consultant values are ignored, factored out of the process, informed choice is restricted, because the client either has not been made aware of alternative values and their possibilities for action, or he has not been made aware of the value implications of the choices he makes.

The dilemma faced in managing OD is how to promote conscious choice by making the consultant's values explicit and simultaneously to preserve free choice by not allowing them undue influence. One effective solution is to define the consultant's role in the OD effort as that of a full and equal organization member, no more and no less. The consultant has specialized skills and values which will influence his opinions on organizational issues. These will be called upon, just as the skills and values of other organization members are called upon to effect the OD program.

The function of the consultant is to use his skills and values to help clarify issues for the client and to offer the organization possibilities of choice which may not have occurred to it, or which might not have been available to it except for the OD program. The consultant has the right and, indeed, the obligation to present a case for lines of action which appeal to him, just as do other members of the organization, but only lines of action acceptable to the group are pursued. In addition to employing his skills and values in this manner, the consultant should be expected to train the client in OD skills so that the process may become a regular, continuing organizational function. This, too, is a unique application of consultant skills in an OD effort, yet it is the embodiment of the fundamental OD concept of "learning through doing." As the members of the organization work with the consultant, they learn from him the skills necessary to perpetuate the effort. In effect, one aim of the OD consultant is to work himself out of a job! These prescriptions of the manner and intent of the application of consultant skills and values set the psychological contract in OD apart from consultancy contracts in other managerial functions.

Completion of the contract is the final step in establishing the charter. At this point, the manager has defined in operational terms who will participate in the OD program, why they are participating, and in a general way how they will participate. This clear definition of the charter and its various components is essential to managing OD effectively. Fundamental as it may be, however, a definitive charter is not in itself sufficient to ensure that an OD program will be an effective one; to complete the context of the OD effort an additional managerial action is needed in the form of legitimation and sponsorship.

PHASE 3. LEGITIMATION AND SPONSORSHIP

The charter established by the OD team must be accepted by a sufficient number of persons, as well as at appropriate levels, of the larger organization to make effective organizational change possible. The OD program must also be legitimated and sponsored.

As we indicated earlier, an OD program need not be initiated at the top levels of the organizational hierarchy. It begins where the manager brings together members interested in gathering information and taking action on organizational issues. This may be at upper management levels, but just as frequently it occurs at middle or lower levels, and often it cuts across levels. The legitimation of the right to examine and to take action on organizational issues is essential if the OD effort is to proceed. The means to proceed must be also made available. Here we refer to such conditions favorable to OD as freedom to admit to the existence of and explore problems, encouragement to experiment, provision for exchange of ideas, and, very importantly, time to participate in all these. This requires the active sponsorship of OD by all those in positions to provide these conditions. Without such support the manager neither can nor should proceed with OD.

In order to secure legitimation and sponsorship for its efforts, the OD team must have access to groups and influential individuals who can provide these. Four basic types of groups and/or individuals may be involved: (1) those whose approval gives sanction to the actions of the OD team; (2) those whose active sponsorship is necessary for establishing facilitative conditions and mobilizing necessary resources; (3) those who remain neutral to the program; and (4) those who oppose the program. In every organization are people who are neutral or opposed to the OD program. While it will be difficult to engage the active support of these people, it is important that the OD team have access to them so that their arguments are constructively inputted into the process. For inclusion of opposing viewpoints may legitimate the effort in the eyes of neutral and opposed organization members.

Ideally, and often, these groups and the legitimation and sponsorship they grant are contained wholly within the membership of the OD team. If not, access to them may be obtained directly by team members through their formal positions in the organization, or, if this is not possible, indirectly through the relationships of team members to other individuals and groups which have more direct access. The selection of means for securing the requisite legitimation and sponsorship is largely a question of individual cases, varying with the situational character of the OD team, its composition, and the broader organizational context. In any case, the choice is the manager's, and his insight into organizational politics is his greatest asset in this phase of managing OD.

Two generally applicable observations can be made about securing legitimation and sponsorship. The first, implied above, is that the broader the membership of the OD team, the greater the access to sources of legitimation and sponsorship. Second, the more clearly defined the charter is, the greater the likelihood that the necessary authority and support will be forthcoming. Those in positions of authority are understandably unwilling to support programs about which they know very little. A well-defined charter, replete with statements of needs, goals, and justification, leaves little question about what activities are being authorized and supported. The consultant, drawing on his experience with other groups, can bring these general guidelines and the alternative means of access to key people to the attention of the OD team and the manager, who with their practical knowledge of the organization can select the means best for their situation.

Once the OD program has been legitimated and provision for its support made, phase 3 ends and the context of managing the OD program has been completed. While they are described here as separate, distinct, and sequentially ordered phases, in practice convergence of interest, establishing the charter, and legitimation and sponsorship seldom follow this precise pattern. Generally speaking, these phases flow into one another and occur more simultaneously than sequentially. This is particularly true of the second and third phases, for legitimation and sponsorship influence the nature of the charter. Regardless of the precise pattern, however, once it has the license to proceed with its efforts the OD team should turn its attention to the program itself, the action step cycle, and to the first step in that cycle, problem identification.

PHASE 4. PROBLEM IDENTIFICATION

It is important for the organization, if it is to improve, to identify the attitudes, behaviors, and circumstances which account for where it is and/or hinder its moving forward. It must identify its problems. In addition to providing a starting point for beginning work, problem identification also serves as an initial and important diagnosis of organization members and their skills, levels of perception, attitudes toward their work, and especially their capacity to accept change in attitudes and work behaviors. It is (or at least it can be) the locus of considerable training activity as well as diagnosis.

The temptation in problem identification is to proceed too casually. The individual members of the OD team bring with them, in addition to their personal motivations, their own views of what is wrong with the organization and where its problems lie. To accept these personal agendas as testimony to organizational problems is to ignore the important criteria of problem identification. The more comprehensive process that is required combines research and action in analysis and fact-finding, as described below.

Successful problem identification, like effective goal setting, meets certain criteria. First, the problems must be important to the person naming them and also significant for organizational functions. Second, the problems must be manageable. Third, problem statements must reveal some fundamental dimensions of causes and effects, so that solutions can be addressed to these fundamentals rather than to superficialities. These criteria dictate (1) that the identification of problems extend beyond the OD team's and the manager's immediate concerns to include the concerns of the widest possible membership of the organization, (2) that such a search be directed to significant problems, and (3) that the data be reviewed in a manner leading to further action.

Thoughtful planning of the problem-solving phase therefore involves the considerations raised in our earlier discussion of diagnosis. (1) What conditions should prevail to allow and to encourage organization members to state problems of importance to them? (2) What kinds of questions about organizational problems should be asked of organization members? (3) What is the best method for fact-finding, for gathering problem identification data, and for translating it into operational, action-oriented form?

The OD team must establish at the outset of the problem identification phase in what context and under what climate organization members will bring significant problems to the surface. Involved here are not only questions of form (interview, questionnaire, group focus, and so on) but also factors of timing and levels of perception. The consultant is responsible for bringing to the attention of the OD team the various means of data collection and their associated variables and for training organization members in their use. The choice of specific methods is, of course, the decision of the manager and the OD team. One important general guideline is that the method used must maintain the security and self-respect of organization members while it yet challenges them to explore their experience within the organization.

Once the form and content of problem identification are chosen, the remaining steps are to conduct the research and assess the resulting data. Here, the training of the OD team often becomes explicit and extensive. The process proceeds at a pace that seems appropriate for the skills of the OD team and the organization members' receptivity to data collection.

An important note should be added here. Research in an OD program is not scientifically rigorous or pure, nor is it intended to be. It is designed and executed in a manner which generates the data necessary to change the system. Therefore everything in the OD process, including problem identification, should contribute to the improved use of internal resources. Objections to the design of the problem identification process from a scientific standpoint are immaterial if the process is valid under the major criterion applied to OD processes: "Is it good for the organization?"

The data gathered during this "fact-finding" step are examined for indications of significant problems which are manageable. Again, in reading these "facts" the OD team will doubtless need guidance and training from the manager and the consultant. Of particular importance are indications of the fundamental causes of attitudes, behaviors, and circumstances that have been labeled problems. It is indications of this sort that will shape the general plan of the OD effort and point the way for subsequent action, for as the fact-finding step of the problem identification phase proceeds, the general plan begins to emerge.

PHASE 5. THE GENERAL PLAN

Evaluation of data from the problem identification phase leads first to a review and any necessary modification of the OD team goals. This allows the group to consider again whether its goals are important to enough people in the organization to evoke general commitment to their achievement. Evaluation of the data also leads to an overall plan of what needs to be done to reach the objective. The plan indicates the problems which must be confronted if the program goals are to be achieved. Finally, evaluation of the data, as well as evaluation of the fact-finding as an action, indicates how these problems may be confronted. These last two items, what to do and how to do it, constitute the general plan of the OD program.

The general plan is a tentative course of action in a sequence of logical steps. Indications of how the plan should be pursued emerge not only from the statements of what problems exist, but also from evaluation of the impact of the fact-finding on the organization and of its implications for subsequent actions. We earlier noted that problem identification serves to provide initial diagnoses of organization members. These diagnoses accrue from members' response to research questions and to the act of research, itself. When asked to cooperate, are members eager or reticient? Helpful or hostile? Supportive or resistive? These reactions, whether favorable or unfavorable to the OD effort, must be introduced into the general plan to allow for their impact on the probable success of alternative approaches to organizational problems.

This evaluation of the fact-finding as action requires insight and analysis. The consultant and the manager must facilitate the difficult process of formulating a general plan by drawing attention to varying interpretations of the data, and they also must train team members in data interpretation. The manager has the additional responsibility of seeing that all the data gathered by the OD team is presented to all the members of the organization.

The general plan is activated after the formulation of an action hypothesis which can be tested, which is the next step in the OD process.

PHASE 6. ACTION HYPOTHESIS

An action hypothesis predicts that certain desirable consequences will result from specific actions. Each action hypothesis, therefore, implies that a desirable goal exists and that there is a means of achieving the goal. Action hypotheses thus operationalize the "what" and the "how" of the general plan.

Developing an action hypothesis requires isolating one of the causal relationships underlying the general plan and hypothesizing alternative courses of action and their impact on the attitude, behavior, or condition isolated: "Given such-and-such a condition, if we do X, we can expect Y to occur." Such hypotheses should not be random but should be guided by managerial considerations of visibility of the action and probability of its success. If the OD program is to have a multiplier effect and be perpetuated in the functioning of the organization, its initial efforts should be both visible and successful.

Under these criteria, initial action hypotheses may not deal with problems that appear to be most critical or of the highest priority. Initially, attention to such determinants of successful action as timing and the availability of appropriate resources may take precedence over priority. In subsequent action step cycles the emphasis in selecting action hypotheses shifts to their significance, as opposed to the assurance of success.

Following selection and development of the action hypothesis, an action plan is formulated and the appropriate resources are marshaled for action. Different actions will, of course, require quite different knowledge, skills, and talents, and the manager and the OD team must be constantly sensitive to the kinds of resource needs they have and also be creative and systematic about discovering the resources when they are needed. Where the appropriate resources are unavailable, the action hypothesis must be rejected.

Generally speaking, the resources needed will be the skills and expertise contributed by members of the group itself, by those linking members of the OD team and outsiders who may be involved, and by groups outside the organization. In the initial action step cycles of an OD program action hypotheses which draw on skills and knowledge held by members of the OD team are more likely to be successful. Organization members are usually more receptive to action initiated by co-workers than by outsiders. Once the action hypothesis is selected and formulated and the appropriate resources are identified and marshaled, the action plan begins.

PHASE 7 AND PHASE 8. ACTION STEP AND FORMATIVE EVALUATION

The action step and formative evaluation phases are described together here because they should occur simultaneously in the OD process. The action hypothesis is tested as the plan of action is executed and data on the success or failure of the plan are collected. These data are carefully evaluated, and if the plan of action needs modifying, the necessary changes are made and the revised plan is tried out. Again data are collected and evaluated and necessary revisions of action made.

In this way each step in the evolving plan is built on the results attained in the preceding step. Such a procedure allows for the use at each step of the study of new insights gained for improving the situation in which the original problem appeared. Specific actions will usually follow the form of one of the approaches to OD introduced earlier and vary accordingly in form and function. Regardless of the specific form of the action steps, the management of the OD process should be similar.

Every action in the OD process is evaluated and the data fed back into the process to check the appropriateness of problem identification, general plan, action hypothesis, and actual plan in action step cycle 1. This same process provides for simultaneous problem reidentification, general plan modification, and action hypothesis phases of action step cycle 2. Phase 9 is not separately considered because it is actually nothing more than a conscious team decision that one action step cycle has been completed and another will be begun.

This way of using data has been termed *formative evaluation* to distinguish it, in nature and intention, from the more customary *summative evaluation*. Formative evaluation, characteristic of managing OD, occurs simultaneously with action and serves the needs of program improvement; it is a continuous process of making assessments of action and reacting to them. Summative evaluation follows action and is an appraisal of the final product or end result. Formative evaluation gives OD its effective adaptability.

Consecutive cycles of plan-action-evaluation/plan-action constitute the OD program. It is a managerial program, or more correctly a managerial *process,* which has no terminus. Organizational improvement should always be an issue for all organizations, for even when things are going well they could be improved. The specific actions taken and the problems to which they are directed will alter, of course, as some problems are solved and new issues emerge. As organization members learn through action and become increasingly competent in the skills of OD, the consultant detaches himself from the process and the organization assimilates OD as a continuing function. James D. Thompson shares this vision of OD as a regular organizational activity when he writes:

> It is possible to conceive of monitoring behavior which scans the environ-
> ment for opportunities — which does not wait to be activated by a prob-
> lem and which does not therefore stop when a problem solution has been
> found. We shall refer to this as *opportunistic surveillance,* and suggest
> that it is the organization counterpart to curiosity in the individual.[2]

[2] James D. Thompson, *Organizations in Action* (New York: McGraw-Hill, 1967), p. 151.

There are in Thompson's "opportunistic surveillance" many of the characteristics one would attribute to OD at its maturity in an organization. In its form and function OD may depart radically from other organizational processes. To internalize the OD process to the extent that it becomes a natural organizational function, the manager and the organization must be committed to instituting a new organizational process. Such a commitment cannot be undertaken without a full review of the associated benefits and costs.

The selection of an appropriate approach to OD involves a variety of considerations. Those approaches which appear to be best suited to the problems and conditions of the client organization are singled out. Final selection from among these alternatives follows after consideration of their respective advantages and disadvantages, which have been discussed earlier. Here we turn attention to the relative merits of the model for managing OD presented above.

AN EVALUATION OF THE OD MANAGEMENT MODEL

Earlier we referred to the basic requirements of OD activity as identified by Chris Argyris: valid information, free informed choice, and internal commitment. Argyris also describes the several tests for checking the validity of information upon which interventions are based. In increasing degrees of power, these tests are public verifiability, valid prediction, and control over the phenomena. Each of these tests is an integral design component of the model for managing OD, to ensure that information which shapes the process is valid and useful.

The first check on the validity of information, public verifiability, refers to the extent of agreement upon data. Ideally, organizational functioning will be described in similar ways—that is, the same diagnosis will come from a variety of sources. The problem identification phase of managing OD constitutes such a check. The information generally accepted throughout the organization as problems becomes the foundation for the general plan and the choice and design of the action step.

The second test, valid prediction, means the ability to make, on the basis of the diagnosis, predictions that are subsequently confirmed. This testing of predictions and hypotheses is precisely what occurs in the OD management model presented here.

The third check, control over the phenomena—or, more to the point, the systematic altering of factors and prediction of the resulting effects on the system as a whole—also is a function of the action hypothesis and subsequent steps of our model. The action hypothesis predicts that if X is done, it will have Y effect on a given attitude, behavior, or circumstance. In the action step phase, if the Y effect occurs when X is done the hypothesis is confirmed and the information at its foundation is validated. If X is done and the Y effect does not occur, this outcome is fed back into the process and the problem is reidentified, which initiates a subsequent action step cycle and another review of the validity of information. Thus every phase of managing the OD process is designed to ensure the generation of valid useful information, with built-in checks to see that the process does, in fact, operate in this manner.

The same is true of the model for OD management in relation to the second criterion of effective interventions, the presence of free informed choice. Free choice implies that the locus of decision making is in the client system, thereby making it possible for organization members to maintain the autonomy of their system and retain responsibility for their destiny. The inherently participative character of our model for managing OD is designed to preserve the free choice of the client; in all phases, from the convergence of interest through the action step cycle, the initiative in OD lies with the client.

Freedom of choice is meaningless, however, if the manager is not aware of the objectives and consequences of his choice at the moment of decision. Choice must be informed to be fully free. This design of the management process seeks to ensure informed choice by placing on the consultant the responsibility for making the client aware of available alternatives, for advocating the alternatives he himself favors, and for training the client in the generation and execution of alternatives. Each of these consultant activities enhances the client's cognitive map of what it wishes to do, thereby contributing to its free informed choice.

The final criterion of effective intervention, internal commitment, means the course of action or choice has been accepted by each member to the point that he has a feeling of ownership and responsibility concerning the choice and its implications. This internal commitment can be evoked through participation in the choices. When OD is managed effectively, participants have a strong feeling of ownership and responsibility toward choices made in the program because they make the choices. Such participation should be evident in every phase of the OD process. The real participation of all those responsible for initiating organizational action and all those obligated to respond ensures the development of the strong commitment required for effective intervention.

The criteria of effective interventions are integral design components of this OD management model. This is a dividend, in large part, of the essential participative character of managing OD, which allows for the regular validation of information, ensures free choice, and develops internal commitment.

It is paradoxical that participation, the source of the model's strength as a way of managing OD, should also prove to be its weakness. For the degree and nature of participation required to manage OD effectively under this model may present problems for the manager contemplating its use. In organizational circumstances with which the required participation would be incompatible, this model for management of OD must be rejected.

Effective OD management requires participation throughout the organization. This is not compatible with the structure of authority in most organizations. Several authors have pointed out the dysfunctional developmental consequences brought on by the inherent incompatibility of a participative model with a situation in which administrative authority unavoidably remains with the top administrators. This not only thwarts the immediate developmental effort but also creates conflicts and tensions which, if not released, seriously threaten the maintenance of the system.

A popular argument in the current organizational literature is that OD and the participation it engenders will reduce differences in organizational power and influence and thereby, in the long run, enhance development. It is surprising that there have been so few empirical investigations to support or refute this popular contention. It is evident that broad participation alone does not lead to power equalization. This suggests that an extended OD effort in an incompatible organizational environment may not enhance development. Greater participation often provides the more powerful with an opportunity to exercise their influence over the less powerful, which increases rather than equalizes power differences.

The statement that participation in decision-making processes by the less powerful leads to a reduction of power differences is invalid as a general assertion. Allowance and provision for participation in OD through effective management do not ensure that real participation, and the dividends associated with it, will be forthcoming.

Two prerequisites for effective participation in decision making are that members be motivated to participate, and that they possess sufficient skill and expertise to do so effectively. Where either the desire to participate or sufficient skill to effect that desire is absent, evidence indicates that, given the opportunity, members will reject involvement in decision making. Many managers have rightfully felt frustrated in their attempts to involve employees who are neither capable nor desirous of participating. Does this imply that where the motivation, skill, and opportunity to participate are not present OD must be summarily rejected? No. But it does suggest that the requisite conditions for effective participation must be developed before the OD program can be initiated and effectively managed. This means strengthening members' motivation, developing participation skills, and making the authority structure receptive to the idea of shared review of information and action. At this point the manager and consultant must address a key question: Do the benefits accruing from OD warrant the considerable effort and perhaps extensive changes necessary to manage the program effectively? In answering this key question accurately and with conviction, managers may be aided by reviewing a case in which OD was effectively managed. Chapter 8 presents such a case.

The Building Service Products Organization Development Case

Building Service Products (BSP)* is a 17-year-old firm which supplies maintenance and janitorial materials to building service companies throughout the Northeast. For the last five years BSP has averaged gross annual sales of $8.5 million, with 1971 the highest at $9.9 million. BSP is a privately held corporation employing 155 men and women. The president, Ernest H. Rummer, started the company in his garage and has been its only chief executive officer. He has grown with the company and is highly respected as a manager in the community and in the industry. He belongs to several professional associations and prides himself on keeping up to date with development in management theory and practice.

In 1972 and the first quarter of 1973 BSP had a severe downturn in sales. Rummer, troubled by this sales slippage, reorganized the sales force and in the process found that discontent over a variety of managerial and supervisory issues was widespread in the workforce. Out of concern that he might be acting too hastily, without sufficient and appropriate data, Rummer decided to withhold organizational changes until a comprehensive review of the BSP climate could be completed. At this point he contacted a consultant from the business school of a university in his area.

THE FIRST THREE PHASES

As was noted in Chapter 7, the steps in effectively managing OD are more likely to blend together than to appear as discrete events, as was the case with

---

*The firm described in this chapter has been thoroughly disguised. The process is an accurate record of what occurred in the OD program, but the location, industry, financial data, and names of personnel have been altered to ensure the privacy of the client.

BSP. (Phase 1. Convergence of Interest, Phase 2. Establishing the Charter, and Phase 3. Legitimation and Sponsorship followed each other in rapid succession.) Over lunch Rummer described the history of BSP to the consultant, who agreed to work with BSP provided it selected an OD team composed of management, supervisory, and nonsupervisory employees, agreed on the psychological contract, and set realistic goals.

The OD management team came together on March 1 to begin the OD effort with the consultant. Members of the team were those who had responded to an open memo from Rummer to all employees informing them of the impending data collection program. The initial meeting was attended by 31 people. Of these, 10 (3 management, 3 supervisory, 3 nonsupervisory, and Rummer) were picked by the group to act as a steering committee, with the remaining 21 to be involved as needed. The consultant and the steering committee finalized the contract and set the goals. The goals put forth for the BSP OD program were:

- To gather and share information on the organizational climate at BSP.
- To train BSP employees in gathering data and sharing skills.
- To recommend the organizational changes in BSP structure, policy, and procedures indicated to be necessary by the data.
- To receive a written response from management to each recommended change.

The goals were recognized by all as important to BSP and as realistic. Rummer echoed management's support by providing the necessary legitimation and sponsorship for the project with a second open memo to all employees citing the goals and general plan of action for the OD effort.

PROBLEM IDENTIFICATION

The steering committee agreed that data collection should begin immediately and supported the use of questionnaires and interviews. From this point on elements of the case can be followed through BSP correspondence, which will give a clearer picture of the day-to-day management of an OD program. Here is the consultant's memo to OD team members setting up the meeting to review the collection process.

DATE: March 5, 1973

TO: Organization development team members

SUBJECT: OD team briefings

We need to get together twice during the next two weeks to begin the process of data collection.

Next Friday, March 9, the team will go over administration of the survey. The survey will be ready for distribution.

On Friday, March 16, I will walk the team members through the interviewing process. This meeting will probably last two hours.

Both meetings are scheduled for the Conference Room at 2:00 p.m.

Thank you for your continued support in this project.

The steering committee had decided that a combination of questionnaire and interview methods would be the most effective and efficient data collection process. It felt that the questionnaire would provide a broad base-line picture of the BSP organizational climate at minimum effort, threat, and cost, while interviews with randomly selected employees from all levels would allow in-depth pursuit of critical issues.

The people effectiveness survey was chosen as the survey instrument after a review of several lengthier and more sophisticated questionnaires. The PES had been widely used in industries and government in the city where BSP was headquartered. The steering committee was impressed by this and by its brevity and simplicity. The interview schedule shown here was one frequently used by the consultant. Again the steering committee was impressed by the effective history of the schedule, its brevity, and its simplicity.

INTERVIEW QUESTIONS

1. What do you believe are the major functions of your job and department?

   (a)   What ways are there to find out what's going on around here?

[Elicits specific information about his task. His view of his task as well as his feelings about it reveal, in essence, his occupational self-image. Does he see himself as being concerned with the larger organization goals? Shows how he fits in. Describes connections and their reliability in the organization.]

2. What do you consider the good features of your job, the department, the organization, that should be preserved and advanced?

    (a)   What do outsiders think of your department?

[How do you like it here? Looks at support functions available in the organization. Reveals things most important to people's effectiveness.]

3. How do you find out how you are doing?

    (a)   What happens when problems come up?
    (b)   How much and what kind of training do people get?

[This often reveals the feedback mechanisms operating within the organization and suggests the nature and quality of supervisor-employee relationships. (a) tells whom people turn to for support and also involves their relationship to supervisors. (b) shows how much training the employee would like to have and how much he depends on the organization to make him into something.]

4. What are some areas of concern to you which might be examined in an effort to improve BSP?

    (a)   How do these pertain to your personal situation in the organization?
    (b)   To the organization as a whole?

[Surfaces abrasive concerns and needs as he sees them, factors that keep him from being effective.]

5. Suppose you were asked to make some plans for this department over the next six months, one year, or five years. What do you think would be the most important things to consider?

[Deals with the most important problems the organization faces and how widely they are known, thought about, and realistically assessed. It asks how much the person is involved in the realities of the organization and relationships within it.]

    At the meetings on March 9 and 16 with the full 31-person OD management team, the consultant reviewed in detail the administration of the questionnaires and interviews. The team decided to brief all employees about the process and provide opportunities for them to ask questions prior to the administering of questionnaires and the conducting of interviews, all to be done on company time (important evidence of management's support of the program). Assignments of responsibility for presenting the briefings, distributing and gathering the questionnaires, conducting the interviews, and compiling the data were made on a voluntary basis. The OD management team committed itself to completing the problem identification phase of the program no later than April 15.

Briefings were held with all work units and all shifts. It was generally felt that they went very smoothly, with considerable questioning but very little outright resistance or negativism from employees. An important reason for the success of the briefings, which contributed to the high return rate on the questionnaires, was that they were conducted by peers. The briefings managed to create among employees a feeling that their opinions were genuinely sought and would be acted upon by the OD management team. At the end of the briefings, the ODMT gave questionnaires to all employees. (The questionnaire was an adaptation of the People Effectiveness Survey shown in Figure 14.) Employees were told they could complete them on the job or at home and return them anonymously to the office assigned to the consultant.

Of 155 questionnaires handed out, 131 were completed and returned. This extremely high return was viewed as strong positive support of the OD program. The distribution of responses is shown in Figure 25.

The members of the ODMT were very interested in how BSP stacked up against other companies, but the consultant cautioned them against making too much of such comparisons, encouraging them instead to set their own standards. The ODMT members set an acceptable "favorable" response rate of 80 percent. Where more than 20 percent of BSP employees reported dissatisfaction, it was read as an indication of an actual or a potential problem area. Using this criterion, the problem areas identified by the questionnaire data, listed in order of their severity, were:

Insufficient information about quality of work (5)
Insufficient cooperation among work groups (2)
Unfair compensation for work done (13)
Unfairness of management policies (6)
Poor use made of employees' abilities (16)
Lack of opportunities for satisfactory future at BSP (17)
Too many rules hamper productivity (9)
Favoritism shown toward a few (15)
No improvement in working conditions over last year (18)
Poorer fringe benefits at BSP than elsewhere (20)

Figure 25. People effectiveness survey at BSP.

	Strongly disagree	Disagree	Agree	Strongly agree
1. My work is satisfying to me.	4	12	85	30
2. There is not enough coopera-tion between my work group and others we work with.	16	51	38	21
3. There are opportunities in BSP for those who want to get ahead.	4	14	83	27
4. For the jobs in my area, work-ing conditions are O.K.	10	14	89	18
5. We don't get enough informa-tion about how well our work group is doing.	11	47	43	21
6. Many BSP employees I know think management is unfair and would like to see the union get in.	20	46	28	13
7. The BSP retirement plan is O.K.	9	10	76	34
8. I can be sure of a job with BSP as long as I do good work.	5	9	80	33
9. There are too many rules and procedures to follow.	12	73	29	11
10. I have as much freedom as I need to do my job well.	7	14	79	28
11. I feel free to tell my super-visor what I think.	11	9	73	37
12. I am proud to work for BSP.	4	7	77	39
13. I am paid fairly for the kind of work I do.	20	31	62	14
14. During the past six months I have looked for a job out-side BSP.	36	65	14	6
15. Favoritism is a problem in my area.	25	61	22	19
16. Most BSP employees are in jobs that make good use of their abilities.	9	31	68	11
17. My job seems to be leading to the kind of future I want.	13	29	69	17
18. BSP is a better place to work than last year.	12	18	66	24
19. I understand what is expected of me in my work.	5	7	83	35
20. Compared with other indus-tries, fringe benefits are good.	7	20	74	22

The consultant asked the ODMT to take similar note of the areas in which high satisfaction was reported, especially BSP pride, understanding of job expectations, retirement plan, job security, and advancement opportunities. It was clear that most of the ODMT members were much more interested in probing deeper into their problems than in patting themselves on the back. There was a sense of urgency about getting on with the data collection interviews. Some members were convinced that the coming interview phase would only verify the data already gathered and was therefore unnecessary. They were anxious to press ahead with recommended changes and wanted the interviews out of the way. Still others, mostly managers, wanted to minimize the problem areas and the need for attention. They emphasized and dwelled on the areas of high satisfaction.

This divided response to the questionnaire data disrupted the cooperation that had characterized the ODMT and threatened the entire OD project. After two very heated meetings, the consultant intervened to remind the group of the psychological contract and their prior commitment to a plan for problem identification. Order was restored and it was decided to continue with the original plan of random interviews. The ODMT agreed not to release any data to employees until the interviews were completed.

ODMT members interviewed 34 employees representing all levels of the organization. The interviews seemed to go smoothly, but interviewers often commented on the brevity of responses and the guarded character of the conversations. This observation was verified by the data, which seemed often cryptic and not as revealing as had been hoped, as can be seen in the following examples of selected interview responses:

1. What do you believe are the major functions of your job and department?

Clerk:	To be prompt, punctual, and efficient.
Laborer:	To be conscientious, safety-minded, and dependable.
Truck driver:	Make sure the equipment is working.
Foreman:	Know how to handle people in order to get the job done.
Manager:	Doing the job right and being responsible.
Draftsman:	A good, well-thought-out solution, fast; a logical clear schedule of jobs and good communication.
Manager:	Do a good job, a neat job, as fast as possible.
Foreman:	Ability to learn, lead, and produce results.
Porter:	Make sure that the equipment is in order.
Supervisor:	Concern, cooperation, and do your job.
Laborer:	Be there every day and doing right.
Truck driver:	Loyalty, sincerity, and honesty.

Truck driver:	Don't know.
Supervisor:	Regular attendance, cooperation, and good work.
Supervisor:	Take care of equipment.
Supervisor:	Good attendance and being nice to the public.
Manager:	Don't make waves, don't suggest new ideas, and never question the boss.

2. What do you consider the good features of your job, the department, the organization, that should be preserved and advanced?

Clerk:	Its employees.
Operator:	Ability to work and unity of fellow workers.
Laborer:	I don't know.
Manager:	The overall unity with which we work.
Manager:	Dedicated top management and area supervisors.
Laborer:	I like friendly people and working outside.
Operator:	I like working with different types of machinery.
Laborer:	The people I meet.
Foreman:	Hours, benefits, and working conditions.
Truck driver:	Casual atmosphere and variety of work.
Lead man:	The results of our work when it is finished. Freedom of choosing your program and techniques.
Supervisor:	The freedom in doing and planning.
Supervisor:	I like outside work.
Supervisor:	Foreman under me.
Supervisor:	Don't know.
Supervisor:	Working together.
Grounds keeper:	I like the working hours and the pay is good.
Lead man:	Area in which I work and association with fellow workers.
Lead man:	Being partially my own boss, working all over.
Porter:	Good benefits.
Truck driver:	Paid vacation, retirement, and outdoor work.
Clerk:	Minimum supervision.
Foreman:	Freedom to make decisions and sick leave.
Foreman:	Being a part of planning.
Foreman:	Experienced employees.
Lead man:	Esprit de corps very good.
Controller:	Pulling together, cooperation and togetherness.
Truck driver:	Unity between supervisors and personnel.
Grounds man:	The people I work with, the work I do.
Manager:	The people in the field, the position, the moving about.

Draftsman:	Security of position, variety of projects dealing with the job itself, and when I can control projects.
Draftsman:	Supervisor's ego.
Manager:	Well-qualified men.

3. How do you find out how you are doing?

Manager:	You don't really know unless you are a favorite.
Draftsman:	Public notice and comment through personal contact and fellow workers.
Grounds man:	They don't say.
Supervisor:	When the boss says that I am.
Grounds keeper:	The supervisor is the first to tell us.
Manager:	I don't usually, but sometimes through the grapevine.
Foreman:	When we are achieving set goals.
Supervisor:	By other people telling me and from 25 years of experience.
Supervisor:	No complaints.
Grounds keeper:	When my foreman is well pleased.
Supervisor:	I don't hear anybody say anything.
Operator:	No way of knowing. Supervisor never compliments.
Grounds keeper:	I am told by my supervisor.
Manager:	You get bawled out and catch hell.
Draftsman:	The immediate superintendent; and persons above him waste no time, energy, or tact in notifying personnel of mistakes.
Grounds man:	They tell you about it.
Supervisor:	Using own judgment.
Clerk.	Few complaints.
Operator:	They never say whether you do good work or not.
Foreman:	Being told.
Supervisor:	Manager will let you know.
Auto equip. oper.:	You will hear about it if it is not done right.
Truck driver:	When I hear gripes and get to do the job over.
Foreman:	Informed by supervisor.
Supervisor:	When supervisor OK's job.
Supervisor:	When nothing is said.
Operator:	When it meets my own satisfaction.
Trainee:	Very little praise is given.
Foreman:	There are no gripes.
Lead man:	When everyone from the general foreman to his supervisor to grounds maintenance tell me I'm not.

Foreman:	We are told about that also.
Supervisor:	By experience.
Supervisor:	Manager jumps on my back.
Operator:	When the supervisor complains.
Supervisor:	When I am told that I am not.
Lead woman:	When they chew me up one side and down the other.
Laborer:	Someone complains.
Custodian:	Supervisor tells you.
Laborer:	They always tell you it's wrong, but hardly ever show you how to do it correctly.
Trainee:	We are never notified of a bad job we have done. Things just slide over.

4. What are some areas of concern to you which might be examined in an effort to improve BSP?

Supervisor:	Uncooperative attitude from crew and equipment maintenance.
Supervisor:	Slow advancement.
Grounds keeper:	My supervisor and his attitude.
Supervisor:	The managers don't give you another chance for another position.
Lead woman:	Training to work a crew that doesn't care about working.
Supervisor:	Salary much too low.
Clerk:	Poor communication between management and myself.
Laborer:	Getting tools back from shop still needing repair.
Supervisor:	The lack of proper materials at the right time to get the job done.
Supervisor:	Too much turnover in employment.
Laborer:	Method of promotions.
Laborer:	Low pay and few raises.
Grounds man:	I don't like getting paid every two weeks. I don't think I'm drawing the right salary.
Manager:	The back-stabbing, orders given, and the handling of different people and things.
Draftsman:	Lack of trust as to professionalism, shifting responsibilities and shifting of job priorities. No control over job planning.
Foreman:	Not enough cooperation from fellow employees. Being treated as if I were a moron. Low pay for the amount of work. The backward way the department is run.
Supervisor:	Not being friendly, not working together.

Custodian:	Too much supervision.
Clerk:	The pay.
Supervisor:	The lack of communication with upper echelon.
Operator:	We need organized coffee breaks.
Foreman:	Not enough help for workload.
Foreman:	Lack of sufficient equipment.
Grounds keeper:	When we begin to fail one another as a group.
Laborer:	Not enough help.
Supervisor:	Budget.
Grounds keeper:	A weak supervisor who pushes his foreman around to do his job.
Leader:	Not informed of what is going on in division as to new policies and new ideas.
Operator:	No communication between supervisor and head foreman.
Truck driver:	Lack of communication between top supervisor and workers.
Lead man:	We could use more manpower.

5. Suppose you were asked to make some plans for this department over the next six months, one year, or five years. What do you think would be the most important things to consider?

Clerk:	More information on training available, job improvement opportunities, and long-range plans for me.
Foreman:	Hire more help, pay better salaries, and give better benefits.
Crew chief:	Better cooperation between crews, to know sooner what we will be working at and what tools we need.
Grounds man:	More money, more benefits, and better working conditions.
Manager:	Ask everybody to do their job, be fair and even-handed with all the employees.
Draftsman:	Reorganizing to eliminate broad overlapping duties, decentralize more of the current organization, assign permanent and distinct responsibilities according to professional abilities.
Foreman:	See that all employees become more knowledgeable in their work, provide incentive pay increases for all employees, and place auto shop under direct supervision of Mr. Anderson.
Truck driver:	Have better supervision.

Grounds keeper:	Hire more employees.
Foreman:	More equipment, four-day work week, more training courses.
Supervisor:	Buying procedures for equipment, better systems, and four-day work weeks.
Truck driver:	Better pay and equipment, and communication from boss to employee.
Lead man:	More help, more experienced manpower, and more interest shown by employees. Staff meetings. Leaders should be given opportunity to learn supervision.
Clerk:	Clerk positions should be upgraded.
Supervisor:	If people could choose co-workers best suited for job. More rapid equipment repairs.
Supervisor:	Get new equipment and have a four-day work week.
Grounds keeper:	Have more meetings to encourage communication.

Despite the brief and cryptic interview responses (a common result with inexperienced interviewers), these data seemed to present a more negative view of the BSP organizational climate than that disclosed by the questionnaires. When the ODMT met to review the interview data, tensions and tempers once again flared. There were sharp divisions between team members over the validity and meaning of the data. Management, while not ignoring clear evidence of BSP problems, was defensive about some of the direct ("accusatory," in their words) statements made in the interviews. Nonsupervisory members of the team, inferring management's motivations, wanted to make more of the problems than seemed to be warranted by the data. Divisive debate once again threatened the entire OD effort.

To bring the problem identification phase to a constructive conclusion, the consultant suggested dividing the ODMT membership into management and nonsupervisory groups for the purpose of clarifying their conceptions of the key organizational issues at BSP as they were revealed through the interviews and questionnaires. Each group met with the consultant under the observation of the other group in a "fishbowl" discussion. First the management group met, with the nonsupervisors as observers, watching but not interfering with their discussion. Then the process was reversed. The "fishbowl" technique is an excellent way to present alternative perspectives on a problem without disruptive conflicting input.

The "top ten" issues in the eyes of each group are listed as follows.

Managers' List	Nonsupervisors' List
There is little knowledge of the "big picture" in the organization.	Top management is not very aware of problems faced at the working level.
Too many projects are undertaken.	Little opportunity for advancement exists.
Little communication of organizational objectives takes place.	There are a number of organizational policies which do not motivate personnel in the organization.
We don't understand each other's goals and objectives.	We don't sufficiently utilize each other's abilities, knowledge, or experience.
We don't sufficiently utilize each other's abilities, knowledge and experience.	Subordinates' ideas at the lower level of the organization are not sought and used very much.
Management needs to be better organized.	One of our biggest problems is getting along with other people.
There is too much competitiveness between divisions, which tends to build friction.	There is little knowledge of the "big picture" in the organization.
Top management is not very aware of problems faced at the working level.	Certain personality clashes in the organization must be faced.
Subordinates' ideas at the lower level of the organization are not sought and used very much.	Productivity, generally speaking, is well below its potential.
We follow a panic mode of operation.	We don't really listen to each other.

THE GENERAL PLAN

How could the OD management team proceed from these divergent lists of BSP problems? With the ODMT the consultant reviewed the many options available, emphasizing survey feedback and team building as the ones he deemed most viable in BSP. After lengthy discussion, the ODMT rejected team building as the first step. Most members felt that team building focused too much on problems at the managerial level and would not have significant impact on the experience of the average BSP worker. Survey feedback seemed to offer opportunities for all interested to get involved in the BSP OD effort, which was considered highly desirable by the ODMT. The SF could be followed by TB.

The BSP survey feedback design had three major steps:

1. To present to all employees, in open briefings by the ODMT, all the data collected, with the consultant present to help answer questions.
2. To offer at the conclusion of the briefings written summaries of the data.
3. To invite the employees to participate, on company time, in task forces set up to prepare reports for management analyzing problems and recommending solutions in the following areas:
   General problems (17 members)
   Motivation (8)
   Communication (11)
   Training (4)

In all, 58 employees involved themselves in task force assignments (as indicated by the numbers in parentheses); indeed, several employees participated in two task forces.

The task forces met over a ten-week period, usually for an hour and a half or two hours every two weeks. The consultant was available to the task forces on request and did meet with each of the groups at least once. His primary role was to encourage the groups to be specific about problems, causes, and recommendations. He urged them to adopt a format for their reports similar to that in Figure 26. At the conclusion of its work, each task force chose a representative to work with representatives from other task forces in preparing the final report.

ACTION HYPOTHESIS AND ACTION STEP

Preparation of the final report and its presentation to Rummer and the executive group was the major action step of the OD effort. The report was composed of a series of action hypotheses produced by the task forces. From the completed report, presented in the following pages, many potential action steps are clear.

Figure 26. Task force sample report.

Problem	Causes	Recommendations
New employees are often hired for good jobs that old employees are qualified to fill.	We never know of job openings in other departments, or sometimes even in our own departments.	Post job openings on bulletin boards and explain the procedure for applying for these jobs.
We are often pulled off a job before it's finished and put on another rush job.	Someone up the line panics when a customer complains and switches priorities. Sometimes we run out of parts.	Better planning and more consideration in supervision could correct most of this.
We sometimes read about BSP events in local newspapers before we hear about them.	The information is sent to both the in-house paper and the press. The in-house paper is monthly and the press is daily.	Let employees hear first about BSP events through departmental meetings, bulletin boards, and supervisors.

Good features	Why they are successful
Informality and friendliness among people.	Managers set a good example. We call our managers by first name and don't have to polish the apple.
Interesting work.	They listen to our ideas and give us a chance to use our heads and change jobs if we get bored.

Task force mission

1. To study the surveys and find out what our problems and opportunities are.
2. To find out what causes these problems and opportunities.
3. To recommend what can be done to solve the problems.
4. To find where we are already doing a good job.
5. To ascertain the causes of the successes we are now having.

BSP OD Task Forces Report

The task forces, composed of the people named on the cover of this report, delved primarily into the problem areas brought forth by the people effectiveness survey and subsequent interviews of personnel by members of the organization development management team.

It is the opinion of the task forces that in general BSP is held in high regard by its employees. We found several areas of concern, however, which will be discussed in the necessary detail in our report, and which we feel will help the company to function more smoothly if action is taken to counter the problems that have become apparent.

The problems will be discussed within several general categories. In each category we will list our interpretation of the specific problem and then comment on what action we feel should be taken. In some cases we feel that just pointing out the problem will lead to its solution.

We appreciate your interest and concern in this matter and hope this report of our findings will be of great value in implementing solutions to the problem areas we have found.

General Problems

1. *Lack of orientation to BSP, its organization, and its goals.*
   Implement a program of orientation for both new and old employees which will set forth clearly what the function of each group is in relationship to the other groups of the company and what the goals of the company are. This should stress both personnel and their jobs and the overall goals of the company in a general form. This type of program should take place on a group level with the oversight of company executive personnel.

2. *Inconsistency in the wants of the supervisor.*
   Supervisory personnel should attempt to be consistent in what they expect of the people rather than concentrating on how things should be done and why they should be done that way. The inconsistency leads to frustration of the employees.

3. *Proper planning.*
   Proper planning should be accomplished on a broad scope to allow personnel to finish projects in an orderly fashion without undue shifts in priorities that cause rush jobs to be done, consequently causing mistakes to be made.

4. *Supervisory evaluations of personnel.*
   Both positive and negative evaluations of personnel should be discussed with the people involved. This will tend to eliminate frustrations of not knowing how they are doing in the eyes of the supervisor. The evaluations will help to fulfill people's "ego" needs or, conversely, help them to solve problems which will hinder their future performance.

5. *Supervisors should be and act like supervisors, not workmen.*
   This has become an apparent problem for many of the trades and maintenance personnel. Supervisors should, wherever possible, be allowed to oversee workers and be "troubleshooters." They should help with the work only when their expertise is required. Foremen should be classified as supervisors and thus should not be required to be in uniform or subjected to the same normal course of work as their crews.

6. *Lack of a chain of command.*
   Many areas of the company are presently functioning with little or no "chain of command." We feel this is especially important on the

level of single unit production workers, who need someone to turn to for assistance with problems. This problem may be overcome by a program of orientation on a group level, if it is handled properly.

7. *Lack of consistent, challenging workload.*

Again, proper planning or orientation may be the solution to this problem. Personnel should be challenged to accomplish more than they are assigned and to assume new work when they and their supervisors feel they are capable of it. A large percentage of the personnel felt this way. This also may be the reason a large number of people wanted a different job. Challenge would contribute a lot to an ego boost.

8. *Duplication of effort.*

Proper planning with knowledge of what other persons are doing and what others should be doing seems to be somewhat of a problem. Especially in the shipping areas, people should be held more responsible for their actions. They should not exceed what they are capable of doing.

9. *Favoritism.*

People should be treated as objectively as possible.

10. *Future and potential.*

People should be told what is possible for them in the future of their job and what advancement could be possible for them with proper training. They should be given an opportunity to advance as they are able to accomplish more.

11. *Deadwood.*

There should be an uncomplicated way to eliminate personnel who are not working to capacity in their job or are otherwise causing detriment to the company's or group's capability.

Motivation

1. *Lack of initiative.*

Initiative should be encouraged, within normal bounds, on the part of persons who want to get ahead. They should be helped when necessary and be able to receive benefits, or recognition, for actions beyond what is required of them.

2. *Ego boosts.*

There are very few compliments paid or thanks given for "a job well done." These, however, should be sincere, as a person will recognize falseness. Give people recognition and challenge them to do more.

3. *Challenge.*
   Challenge people to strive to work above what they are now capable of doing, to emulate supervisors, be involved, and so on.

Communication

1. *Feedback.*
   Communication downward from supervisors seems to be good; however, feedback is seldom solicited from employees. Nor do supervisors tend to be willing to listen to ideas from their employees or their counterparts in other divisions and areas.

2. *Talking "down" to employees.*
   This should, if possible, be brought to supervisors' attention and eliminated, as it tends to cut off lines of upward communication.

3. *General comments.*
   Comments made by management in group managers' meetings should be discussed with supervisory personnel in each division. Possibly, copies of the meeting minutes containing division reports could be disseminated to supervisory personnel in all divisions.

Training

1. *Safety programs; general discussions.*
   Safety meetings should be implemented, especially for jobs in which persons may be subjected to danger, such as in shops and operational maintenance. And after each meeting, while personnel are together, have discussions of general goals and problems which may have arisen concerning specific overall group activities.

Conclusion

We have endeavored to "zero in" on problems we have become aware of through the organization development program of the company. We feel that our recommendations, when implemented, will help to solve these problems and create a better company.

As a whole, we feel that the company is a very fine one of which we are proud to be a part. It is our view that, although the specific things we have mentioned seem to be numerous, the company has many more good features than bad ones, and that for such an organization it is outstanding.

It is the recommendation of our group that the task forces be expanded and continued on a regular basis as open lines of communication and coordination between divisions of the company. We recommend that copies of this report of the task forces be distributed to all personnel in the company to demonstrate that action is being taken and will open further channels of communication in the future.

The task force report went to Rummer and the executive group, who were mindful of their prior commitment to respond to employee-generated data. The management group began to meet to review the task forces' work. Starting on July 30, Rummer began to issue on behalf of management a series of memoranda responding to employee problem analyses and recommendations. Several of these contained specific change actions.

DATE: July 30, 1973

TO: All employees of Building Service Products

SUBJECT: Organization development interim report

The task forces have turned in their written report to management for consideration of various suggested changes in the operation of Building Service Products. Many of these recommendations came from the effectiveness survey and interviews which have been conducted during the past several months. To keep you informed of the progress of the organization development program, the following comments are made as a result of the first meeting of the management task force.

Two committees have been established to develop a training program for all employees and supervisors. In the 1973-74 budget we gave approval to hire a training supervisor. The training program will be studied prior to the hiring of this supervisor and could possibly begin by October of this year. The training program will be very detailed, involving many facets of supervisory skills, safety, and specific training relating to individual job requirements.

Another committee was appointed to study and make recommendations for the establishment of orientation sessions. Orientation will be done for all employees presently in the company and all new employees hired in the future. Orientation will cover the company, each group and its relationship to other groups, and the individual employees and where they fit into the program.

These two committees working together will plan and make recommendations on how to provide an effective communications program to keep all employees informed of company activities.

There will also be started group "rap sessions" which will permit instructions and information to be disseminated to employees, and at the same time will provide employees a chance to ask questions involving job, work conditions, personnel problems and procedures.

Educational benefits for employees desiring to better their education will be made known to the entire company.

Although management has so far had only one meeting, many others will be held to work on all of the problems mentioned in the task forces report. Solutions and/or changes will take time, but you can rest assured that we will continue to solve the problems and will keep you advised of our decisions on a regular basis. I feel that the many, many hours spent by our employees in the interview and survey techniques will be rewarding to them and to the company.

Additional reports from me will follow as work on the suggestions progresses.

DATE: August 9, 1973

TO: All employees of Building Service Products

SUBJECT: Report of organization development program task
              forces

The report of the task forces, July 13, 1973, contained several references to personnel policies. This memorandum will be an initial response to the points raised. It is intended to become the basis for mutual discussions to develop more effective programs and to eliminate problems.

Besides those items specifically identified under the personnel heading, other items clearly have personnel implications.

Here are specific comments in reference to the items included in the report.

General Problem #4. Supervisory evaluations of personnel

We concur that evaluations should be discussed with the employees involved. The present evaluation form does not lend itself to discussion and focuses on traits rather than work responsibilities. An alternative concept is being developed. We will soon need to try these concepts out on a broader basis.

General Problem #10. Future and potential

We concur fully. Tuition reimbursement and other training programs are intended to provide an opportunity to advance. Counseling by personnel department staff is available.

General Problem #11. Deadwood

Present procedures for removal of unsatisfactory personnel have been developed over many, many years, and are not as complicated as many people feel. Better training of supervisors may be the way to accomplish this. It is important to retain safeguards against a patronage or spoils system.

Training: Safety programs; general discussions

Personnel shares with each department the responsibility for developing viable safety programs. This responsibility has not been implemented because of staffing inadequacies. A position has been funded in the personnel department effective October 1 to take over this responsibility.

DATE: August 20, 1973

TO: All employees of Building Service Products

SUBJECT: Organization development management report #2

July 30 was the date of the first report, and I stated that additional reports would be forthcoming as progress is made.

1. The first supervisor training course was started on Sunday, August 19, 1973. Some 45 supervisors were in attendance. The course is being taught by the personnel department.

2. Technical training begins the latter part of August, and following the training of supervisors announcements will be forthcoming.

3. Training records of every employee are being established at one central location. This includes formal education, classroom training, and on-the-job training records.

4. Orientation classes for all employees are to begin in early September. These are to be conducted by personnel and supervisors of each division.

5. Codes, technical books, and tools (where appropriate) are available for purchase by the groups that have a need for them.

Many other suggestions are being worked on, and the results will be announced as soon as programs and policies are ready.

A *service incentive* pay plan has been included in the 1973–74 budget. This will provide for salary incentive payments to employees with five or more years of service plus an across-the-board raise for all employees.

Progress is being made, and with all of us pulling together we can overcome all problems.

Other minor changes were made in the ensuing months, but the press of business activity wore away at the intensity of the OD program. In January 1974, approximately nine months after the OD program began, the consultant reminded BSP of the importance of evaluating what had been done.

FORMATIVE EVALUATION

In BSP evaluation of task force recommendations and managerial responses went on constantly in informal groups on the line, in the lunchroom, and in the hallways. After nine months of activity there appeared to be general satisfaction with the entire OD process throughout BSP. The consultant urged a more structured review and was enthusiastically supported by the OD management team. With the support of management, the ODMT reconvened in February 1974 (some former members dropped out, some task force members joined in). In their evaluation deliberations the ODMT reviewed the initial task force report and commented on the progress they felt had been made on BSP problems and their initial recommendations. A new report to management was prepared using the same format. (The new "phase 2" report follows. It can be cross-checked with the first report, which used the same headings.)

General Problems

1. *Lack of orientation to BSP, its organization, and its goals.*
   General program of orientation has been started.

2. *Inconsistency in the wants of the supervisor.*
   These are still problem areas.

3. *Proper planning.*
   When a problem is encountered, all interested people should be included in the planning phase, the group decision should be documented, and then all people involved should stand by the decision. The means of implementation of the decision should be left to the persons involved in accomplishing the project, with only minor guidance (except where requested) from management. As an example, the PM project was changed in scope so many times during its implementation that the critical factor became time, not permanent quality, which it should have been. Rush jobs lead to mistakes, greatly escalated project costs, inferior quality in the interest of speed, or any combination of the above.

4. *Supervisory evaluations of personnel.*
   The monthly evaluation sheets should have a category for punctuality on them. We also recommend doing away with the various objectives in the present grading system and making a new grading system in which the individual supervisor can determine when someone is performing at a satisfactory (or unsatisfactory) level and recommend either a merit increase or no merit increase, without being forced to maintain certain percentages of his department's people at satisfactory, superior, or outstanding ratings. These rating sheets should be filled out by the supervisors without input from higher management levels, as people on the higher management levels can revise the ratings later if they so desire.

5. *Supervisors should be and act like supervisors, not workmen.*
   This item has been partially implemented. In some areas, the "boss" is still expecting his supervisors to do actual repair work all the time,

instead of allowing them to supervise and/or instruct those in their field. Supervisors should be allowed time for planning, instructing, and administrative duties.

6. *Lack of a chain of command.*
    Much improvement has been noted.

7. *Lack of consistent, challenging workload.*
    The area of concern is primarily with stenographers and clerks. We feel that there is a need to create more interest in the workings of the division and department, resulting in workers' better understanding of the kind of work each division does, thereby encouraging people to involve themselves in more meaningful tasks and increase their capabilities and responsibilities. We recommend that managers schedule enrichment projects during the periods of low workloads.

8. *Duplication of effort.*
    This has been partially implemented; however, there seems to be the same problem as before.

9. *Favoritism.*
    No further comments.

10. *Future and potential.*
    This is still a problem.

11. *Deadwood.*
    Further comments will be made later in the report text.

Motivation

1. *Lack of initiative.*
    This is a sensitive area and one where some improvement has been noted. We feel that this is being considered carefully by management and will be even further improved in the future.

2. *Ego boosts.*

3. *Challenge.*

Communication

1. *Feedback.*
    Feedback is much better than before but is still not encouraged in certain divisions. Most supervisors will not listen to this feedback in the first place, and in the second place will discipline the one who dares to speak up. The "rap" sessions promised in the organization development interim report have not been held by any group.

2. *Talking "down" to employees.*
   This problem is still there.

3. *General comments.*
   There is a need for all groups to be informed of future planning at staff meetings. Each division head should be encouraged to bring one or more supervisors to these staff meetings, so that the overall picture can be presented. Not only will this be good training for the supervisors, but it will also be a great help in implementing the departments' goals. Greater understanding of the problems facing all would promote greater cooperation.

Training

1. *Safety programs; general discussions.*
   We feel that this part of the program will be very satisfactorily implemented under the new safety and training manager.

Upon receipt of the ODMT evaluation report Rummer and the management group moved into another action cycle. The report reassessed earlier identification of BSP problems and evaluated progress that had been made on recommended solutions—it became, in effect, an exercise in formative evaluation. Management's response to the second report came in late March 1974 and maintained their commitment to respond to issues generated by OD. Management's response was less thorough but more specific than before.

DATE: March 27, 1974

TO: All employees of Building Service Products

SUBJECT: Organization development phase 2 report

The task force of supervisors and nonsupervisors has had several meetings and, as a result, has presented management with a phase 2 report. This will be available on request from my administrative assistant.

A meeting was held with the combined task force to discuss many features of the report, and I am submitting the following points for your information.

1. Basic communication has improved between supervisors and employees. This must continue to improve, and I am asking each supervisor to conduct informal meetings with employees to disseminate information and discuss problems.

2. Orientation sessions have been held and others are to follow on a regular basis.

3. Supervisory training has been conducted and will continue.

4. Technical training will commence within 60 days. A program of this type takes time to prepare the proper material and its presentations.

5. A safety program is being prepared by an industrial engineer, and should be under way within this year.

6. Performance evaluation sheets are under study and may be changed during the year.

7. Service incentive pay was established and first paid last December. This is a longevity-type pay and rewards the employee for continuing employment.

8. Continuous improvement is being made in delineating requirements between major maintenance and operational maintenance. The preventive maintenance program is a new concept and will take additional time to be fully established and to have its exact functions and goals settled.

9. I am asking the group supervisors to hold their own group meetings to disseminate information and reports coming from the monthly group supervisor meetings.

These items do not answer the entire report but address the most important points. I hope that each of you will discuss this report and these problems with your supervisors.

Much time and effort has been put into the organization development program by employees and management. I feel that progress has been made in making this a better place to work.

In July 1974 Rummer sent to the consultant the following memorandum giving his observations on the OD program at BSP and its contributions to BSP productivity.

DATE: June 7, 1974

TO: [Consultant]

SUBJECT: Organization development program of Building
             Service Products

The organization development study points up needs for orientation of employees, supervisory and nonsupervisory training, consistency in hiring and discipline of employees, safety training, improved communications.

Management has met with the various task forces on two different occasions and we have implemented the supervisory training program and orientation sessions, purchased equipment, provided technical code books and tools, changed working hours, commenced the training program, started on a safety program, improved basic communications by having supervisors meet with their employees, and established meetings in the divisions.

Measurement of productivity is difficult and will vary with the projects undertaken. We definitely see an increase in morale, which has in itself increased productivity in the company. Many items brought to us by the employees are normal management responsibility. Yet I feel that by going through organization development we are able to put many of the programs into effect much faster. It is my personal belief and the belief of my managers that the time and effort spent on this program were justified and can only go to improve the relationship between management and employees, thus making the company a better place to work.

The consultant has not been involved with BSP since June 1974. However, in June 1975 he received from the third ODMT a summary of results from a new personal effectiveness survey made some 18 months after the first one. Figure 27 compares the results of the two surveys. The improvement in the percentage of favorable responses is clearly evident.

Figure 27. BSP employee surveys of 1973 and 1975 compared.

Question	Percent Responding 1973	Favorably 1975
1. Work satisfying	88	92
2. Cooperation among work groups	53	47
3. Opportunity for advancement	86	85
4. Working conditions O.K.	82	90
5. Receive sufficient information about quality of work	48	44
6. Management is fair	62	64
7. Retirement plan O.K.	85	90
8. Have job security	89	86
9. Few rules and procedures to follow	68	72
10. Freedom to perform job well	84	85
11. Can freely communicate with supervisor	85	80
12. Proud to work for BSP	91	96
13. Fairly compensated for work	60	70
14. Not looking for another job	83	87
15. Little favoritism	68	66
16. Good use of employees' abilities	66	71
17. Good job future at BSP	67	74
18. BSP improved over last year	75	83
19. Understand performance expectations	91	92
20. Good fringe benefits compared with other industries	78	90

It is academically risky to assign causes to these changes in employees' views of the organizational climate at BSP over a two-year period. One cannot help being impressed by the realization that the major managerial activity in BSP during the period 1973–1975 occurred around problems identified and solutions recommended through the OD program. This observation, together with Rummer's analysis of the contributions of OD to BSP's performance, points to a generally positive use of OD at BSP.

One final note on this case: BSP sales and profits have been on the increase through 1973 and 1974 and the first quarter of 1975. The ODMT has begun a third phase of its efforts and E. H. Rummer is continually called on by his outside business associates to explain what OD is and how it worked at BSP.

CHAPTER 9

What Goes Wrong with OD ?

Our tone throughout these pages has been both descriptive and prescriptive. We have attempted to *describe* the kinds of information operating managers need to have about OD and the kinds of choices managers need to make about OD and to *prescribe* the way those choices, once made, should be managed. Where these kinds of information, choices, and management plans exist, the result is usually an effective OD program, as it was in the case of BSP. As operating managers know full well, this is seldom the case.

The scenario is all too familiar. The impetus for OD seldom comes from operating managers. More often a staff vice-president "sees the light" at a management seminar and orders that all units reporting to him *will* initiate an OD effort. Many times a consultant convinces top management that OD is just what the company needs and everyone down the line "buys in." Too often the OD project begins without a convergence of interest but, rather, with a coercion of interest.

At some point in the project things begin to go wrong. Where or how is seldom made clear: the consultant is reluctant to assign blame, and sponsoring executives have often lost interest and do not care to find out. The operating manager is left holding the bag, which now contains all of his old problems and usually some new ones, as well.

Managers talk to each other (outside the company more often than in), passing the word of their unsuccessful experiences with OD. This seems the major mode of communicating OD failures, just as publication in the professional literature is the major mode of communicating OD successes. In any event, managers talk to each other about OD, and the talk is seldom flattering; soon OD comes to be regarded as something to be avoided and discarded accordingly. In many companies this has already happened.

There have been, are, and will be OD projects which fail, but these failures, we believe, have more to do with the information, choices, and management of OD in the situations than with OD as a generic managerial practice. In this final chapter we want to suggest why OD sometimes goes wrong and to point out signs to be viewed by managers as red flags in the turbulent seas of organizational change.

Executives, managers, employees, and union representatives are seldom sufficiently educated in the theory and practice of OD. Most often companies start OD efforts without properly educating all those concerned as to what they can expect of OD. Briefings, outlines, and mass presentations are commonplace and often sufficient to "kick off" an OD effort, but they are seldom substantial enough to prompt sustained commitment and investment over time. Where organization members do not clearly understand what is to occur, anxiety increases and is followed by suspicion and soon by resistance, covert and overt. A time-honored axiom among OD practitioners is "communicate before, during, and after change." In OD, communication and education are very nearly synonymous. Figure 28 shows how important information and involvement are to the success of an OD program.

Figure 28. Response to organizational change.

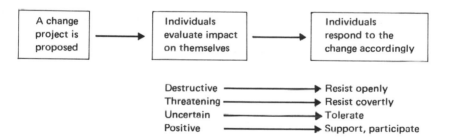

A person's evaluation of the impact a proposed change will have on him usually results from:

1. The amount of information he has about the proposed change.
2. The extent to which he can participate in change project decisions.
3. How much he trusts the initiator of change.
4. His past experience with change.

Adapted from Robert M. Fulmer, *The New Management* (New York: Macmillan, 1974).

Realizing the importance of communicating critical information to employees to educate them to the OD effort, management should see that at least minimally the introduction of OD should include:

- Review of the organization's history of change (to acknowledge past experience).
- Declaration of the initiator's motives and expected rewards (to facilitate trust).
- Extensive review of the theory of OD, its practice in other companies, and the plan for OD in their company (to provide as much information as possible about the proposed change program).
- Explanation of the roles individuals will be expected to play in the change process, including when and for what issues they will have decision inputs (to clarify the extent to which individuals can participate in change decisions).

Where these educational prerequisites are not met, and they usually are not, managers run the risk that their employees are not properly prepared for OD, which jeopardizes the success of the entire change program.

Diagnosis prior to planning and executing OD is seldom systematic and thorough. OD often goes wrong because there is no clear understanding of what needs to be made right! At worst, diagnosis in OD is limited to what top management thinks is wrong or where the consultant thinks he can help. All too often the diagnosis is based on the ideas of individuals at the top, and whatever distortions are manifested in these views are exaggerated on transfer to the total organization. Rarely does the whole organization membership get involved in problem identification and general planning. The common result of these diagnostic practices is that the OD program which emerges deals only with symptoms and does not touch the fundamental organizational problems. Because it deals only with symptoms, little real change is felt or seen by organization members, and they rapidly lose interest in and commitment to the OD effort.

A simple checklist for managers can aid in the development of systematic and thorough diagnosis. At the outset of the OD effort managers ought to ask themselves the following questions:

1. What is the change problem? What are the specific behaviors that need to be altered for this company to move ahead?
2. What are the organizational systems related to this problem? What people, functions, and procedures are involved? How do they interface? Where will changes begin? Where will changes be felt?

3. How ready and able to change are each of these systems?
4. What are our own motives and resources in the situation? What do we hope to achieve, to gain? What are we prepared to commit to bring the changes about?
5. What are the intermediate goals? Setting aside long-term objectives, what will we look for as indicators that things are progressing satisfactorily?
6. Where will we start?

Perhaps the major problem in diagnosing for OD is managerial distortion. Because of the overview of the organization that their position affords, and demands, managers often complete the diagnosis before it is ever begun. The above checklist confronts managers with their own biases and prejudgments about organizational problems. Answering these questions shows managers where they are starting from and provides an important impetus for a more comprehensive diagnosis of the organization.

Where managers are not cognizant of their own distortions of organizational realities, OD efforts often "fix" on problems too early, too narrowly, and too superficially. The result is usually an unsuccessful organizational change experience.

Readiness and capability for change are assumed rather than assessed. It should by now be very clear that an effective OD effort is contingent on many variables, not the least of which are the abilities and inclinations of organization members. Yet, remarkable as it may seem, employee ability and readiness to change are almost universally assumed and rarely ever systematically assessed.

The usual process, once the direction and details of the OD program have been decided, is to ask: How soon can our people have it done? More appropriate questions would be: What are our people ready to change? What are they capable of changing?

As an aid to the manager in assessing organization members' readiness and capability for change is the concept of the "comfort zone." For any area of behavior, whether personal or professional, each individual has a number of behaviors he finds suitable and feels at ease with. These form his "comfort zone." Outside this zone are the behaviors with which he does not or would not feel at ease. People are ready and able to change from one behavior to any other within the comfort zone, but their readiness and capability for change diminish as the situation requires them to move further away from the comfort zone.

From this it can be understood that organizational changes that work within individuals' comfort zones are well received and implemented. Figure 29 shows a plus at position *a* indicating high probability of effective change. The circle at position *b* indicates a 50-50 chance of effective change. Changes that call for behavior far outside the comfort zone (position *c* showing a minus) will probably be unsuccessful.

Figure 29. Comfort zone concept.

To assess the chances for success of contemplated changes, managers must project employee comfort zones by using these variables to estimate the breadth of comfort zones: (1) employees' willingness to take responsibility and risks, (2) employees' education, task competence, and variety of task experience, and (3) employees' motivation.

Where the planned change appears to fall in area *a*, the comfort zone, managers can go ahead at full speed. Where the change effort falls at the margins of the employee comfort zone, success is at best a 50-50 proposition. And where the OD effort requires change in the *c* region, far beyond the boundaries of the comfort zone, managers would be well advised to redirect their efforts, for OD here is almost certain to fail. In these latter instances, *b* and *c* category changes, astute managers turn their attention first to developing the readiness and capability required to effect the needed changes. That is, they concentrate on expanding employee comfort zones before moving ahead with OD. Where the requisite readiness and capability for OD are assumed, rather than assessed, OD stands only a haphazard chance of success.

OD programs are usually managed in the context of the very policies and procedures they seek to change. We know a great deal about change and how to manage it effectively. Some of what we know, like the importance of clear communication, is consistent with existing managerial knowledge and practice. But other things we know about effective change, such as the importance of participation, are not universally found in management practice. The model for managing OD described in Chapter 7 was designed to take advantage of current knowledge about the nature of change and its effective implementation. Implicit in that model is the conviction that managements must change the way they approach the investigation of change at the worker level. Strategies for bringing about change must be consistent with the policy and procedural changes managers are trying to bring about.

We cannot emphasize too strongly the importance of managerial models and rewards as impetus to and support for OD. In the final analysis, it is less the change itself which marks the success or failure of OD than it is the way in which the change is managed. (Employees remember how things were done to them, for them, or with them long after they have forgotten what actually was done.)

In our experience the four factors above have been the major pitfalls in OD programs—they are "what goes wrong with OD." Having been this candid about what goes wrong with OD, is there anything to be said about "what goes right with OD"? The things which make OD work, which make it "go right," are the very things we have emphasized in this book:

1. Full information about OD, its alternative forms, and their strengths and weaknesses.
2. Full understanding of the choices which managers must make in an OD effort.
3. Full understanding of how to manage OD effectively.

These are certainly not panaceas for all that ails OD efforts, but they do seem to be prerequisites for any successful effort.

OD is emerging as an inherent function of management on both external and internal organizational fronts. Externally, changes in the marketplace and the environments of business force concomitant changes in the organization of business. Internally, employees' demands for rehumanization of the workplace and a greater voice in the control and direction of their own work lives force changes in the organization of work. These forces seem destined to increase and intensify despite (perhaps even because of) fluctuations in economic and employment trends.

Responsibility for initiating and effecting these changes will in most organizations fall to the operating managers. The success of their efforts to bring about substantive and positive change rests in large part on their familiarity with and skill in organization development. By contributing to the information base operating managers have about OD and its management, we hope to contribute to their success as effective agents of beneficial change in their organizational arenas.

Index